human body systems worksheets book for kids

BY BASSMA DOUKAR

© copyright

All rights reserved. No part of this book may be reproduced or transmitted in any form or by any means, electronic or mechanical, including photocopying, recording, or by any information storage and retrieval system.

This book belongs to :
_____

Table Of Contents

1. Skeletal System..............4
2. Muscular System..............11
3. Circulatory System..............19
4. Respiratory System..............26
5. Digestive System..............35
6. Nervous System..............44
7. Endocrine System..............53
8. Immune System..............61
9. Urinary System..............69
10. Integumentary System..............77
11. Reproductive System..............85

THE SKELETAL SYSTEM

Name:............................... Date:...../...../..........

Label the parts below:

THE SKELETAL SYSTEM

Name:............................ Date:....../....../..........

Bones Names:

Scapula	Pelvis
Femur	Vertebral column
Radius	Fibula
Sternum	Patella
Thoracic cage	Tibia
Humerus	Phalanges
Carpal	Cranium
Ulna	Cervical vertebrae
Talus	Mandible

THE SKELETAL SYSTEM

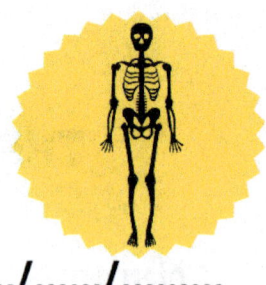

Name:............................ Date:....../....../........

Bone Match-Up:

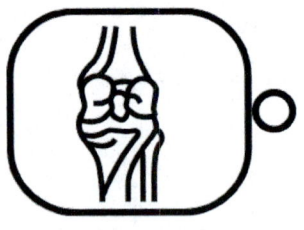

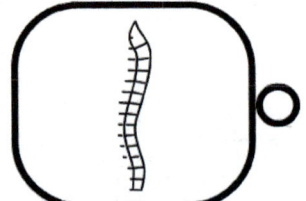

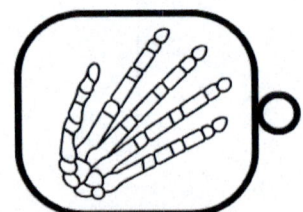

Pelvis
Cervical vertebrae
Thoracic cage
Vertebral column
Femur
Patella
Phalanges
Talus
Cranium
Humerus

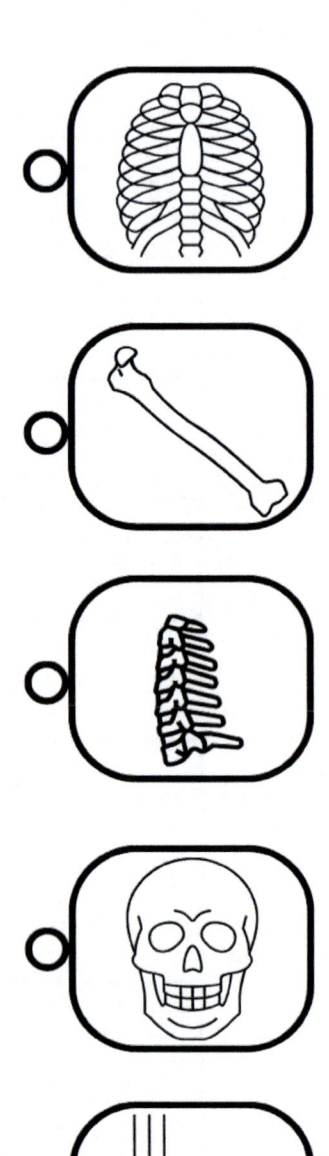

THE SKELETAL SYSTEM

Name:............................. Date:....../....../..........

Bone Functions:

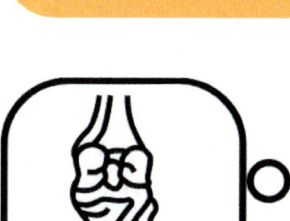 ○ ○ Provides a protective shield for the lower abdominal organs, including the bladder, reproductive organs, and parts of the digestive system.

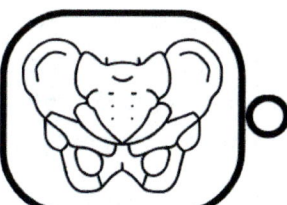 ○ ○ Provide a protective enclosure for the brain, which is one of the most vital organs in the body. Also serves to support the structures of the face, including the eyes, ears, and nose, as well as the muscles of the head and neck.

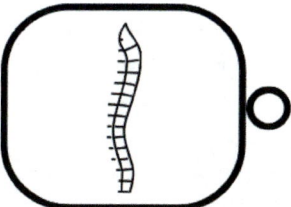 ○ ○ Protect the vital organs of the thoracic cavity, such as the heart, lungs, and major blood vessels.

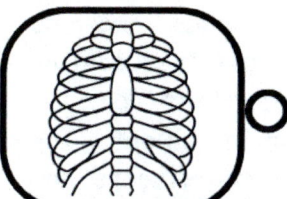 ○ ○ Protect the spinal cord and provide support and stability to the body. It also allows for movement of the head, neck, and trunk and serves as an attachment point for muscles and ligaments.

 ○ ○ Protect the knee joint and improve the leverage of the quadriceps muscles during knee extension.

THE SKELETAL SYSTEM

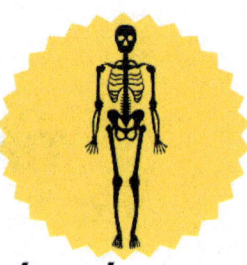

Name:................................ Date:......./......./..........

Bone Functions:

is an important bone in the ankle joint, and it is responsible for several important functions related to movement and stability.

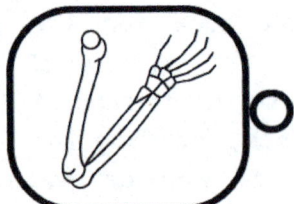
Provides support for the weight of the upper body and helps to maintain an upright posture. Involved in a variety of movements, including walking, running, jumping, and climbing.

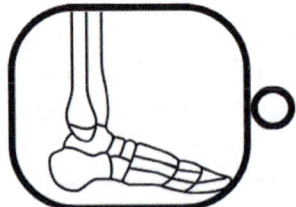
Provides structural support for the upper arm and protects the nerves and blood vessels that pass through it.

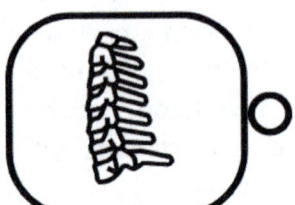
Provide grip and control when grasping objects with the fingers and toes. contain many sensory receptors that provide information to the brain about the position and movement of the fingers and toes.

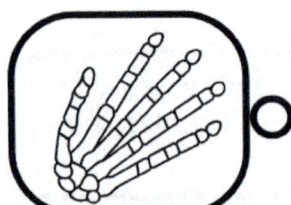
Provide support for the head, which weighs around 10-12 pounds, and allow for the neck's flexibility and range of motion.

THE SKELETAL SYSTEM

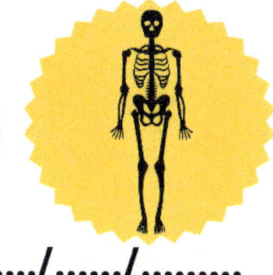

Name:............................... Date:....../....../..........

Bone Diseases:

Bone Diseases	Symptoms	Treatments
OSTEOPOROSIS		
OSTEOARTHRITIS		
PAGET'S DISEASE		
OSTEOGENESIS IMPERFECTA		
SCOLIOSIS		

THE SKELETAL SYSTEM

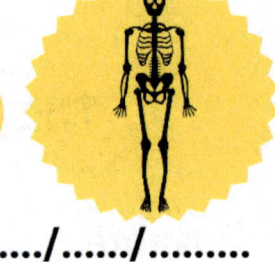

Name:............................ Date:...../...../........

BONES CATEGORY:

BONES CATEGORY	DESCRIPTION	EXAMPLES
LONG BONES		• fumur • •
SHORT BONES		• • carpal •
FLAT BONES		• • • scapula
IRREGULAR BONES		• • pelvis •
SESAMOID BONES		• • patella •

10

THE MUSCULAR SYSTEM

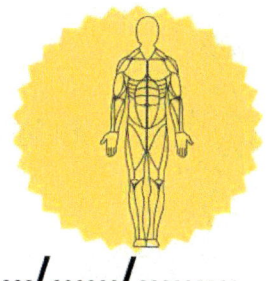

Name:............................... Date:....../......./.........

Label the parts below:

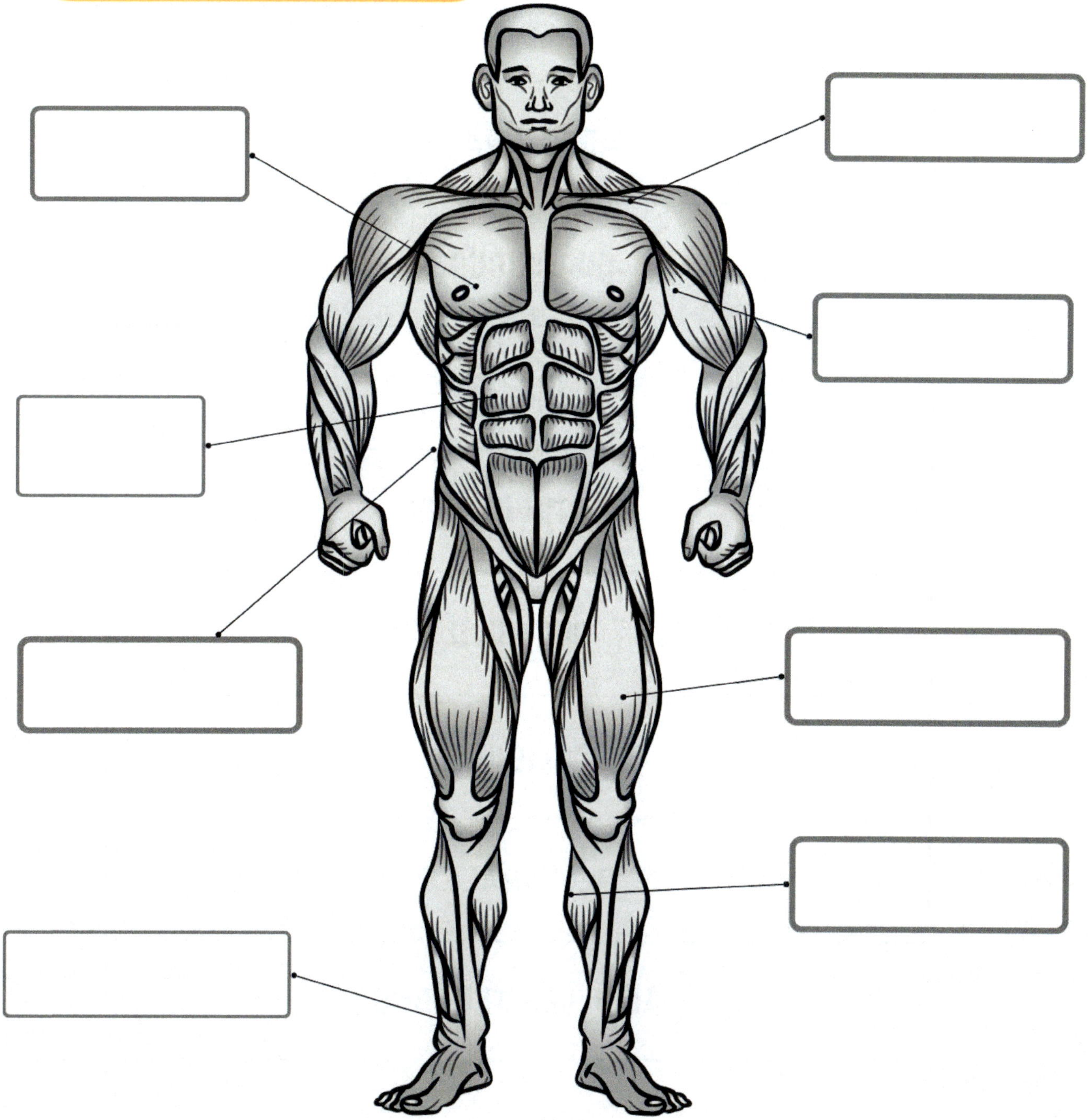

THE MUSCULAR SYSTEM
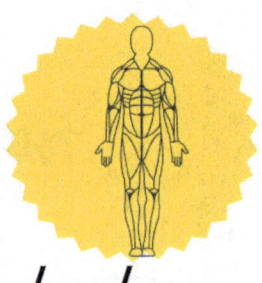

Name:............................   Date:....../....../........

Muscles Names:

ABDOMINALS
QUADRICEPS
BICEPS
GASTROCNEMII
DELTOIDS
OBLIQUES
PECTORALES
ACHILLES TENDONS

THE MUSCULAR SYSTEM

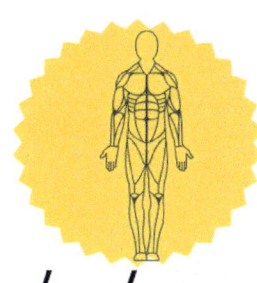

Name:................................ Date:......./......./..........

Muscle Match-Up:

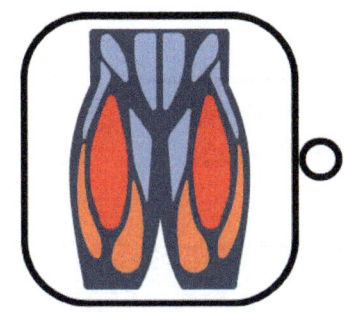

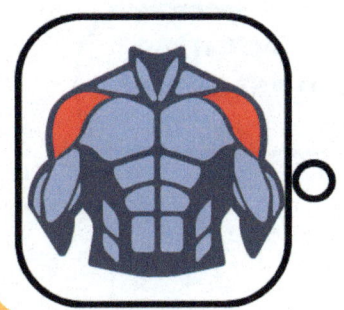

| ABDOMINALS |
| QUADRICEPS |
| BICEPS |
| GASTROCNEMII |
| DELTOIDS |
| OBLIQUES |
| PECTORALES |
| ACHILLES TENDONS |

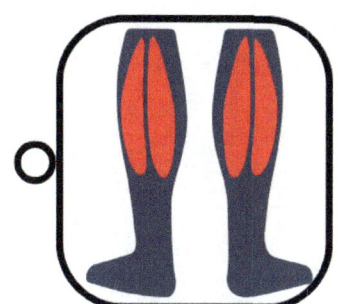

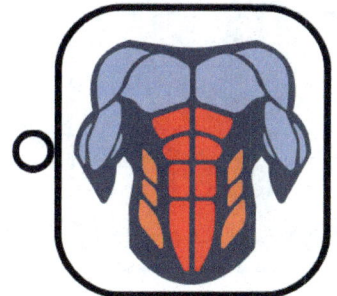

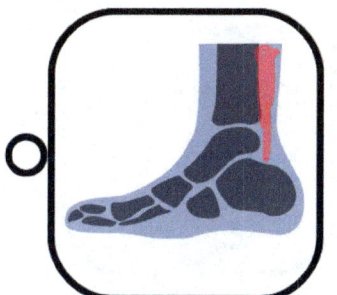

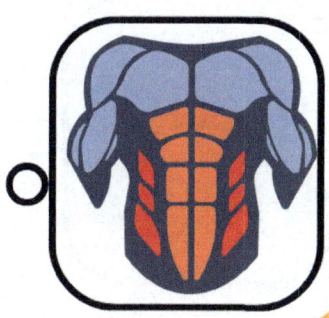

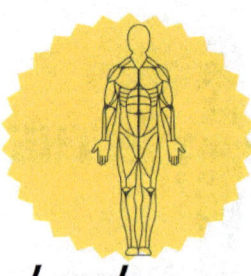

THE MUSCULAR SYSTEM

Name:............................. Date:....../....../.........

MUSCLE FUNCTIONS:

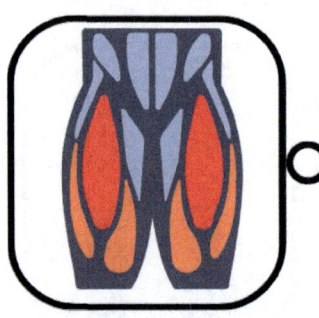

RESPONSIBLE FOR TRUNK FLEXION, LATERAL FLEXION, AND SPINAL STABILIZATION.

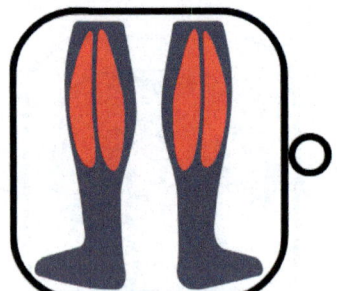

EXTENDS THE KNEE AND FLEXES THE HIP.

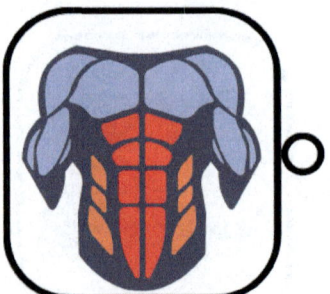

FLEXES THE ELBOW AND SUPINATES THE FOREARM.

PLANTARFLEXES THE ANKLE (POINTING THE FOOT DOWNWARD) AND ASSISTS IN KNEE FLEXION.

THE MUSCULAR SYSTEM

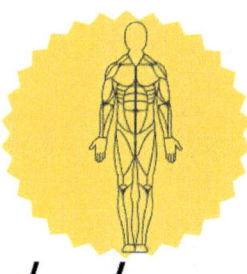

Name:................................ Date:......./......./.........

MUSCLE FUNCTIONS:

ALLOW FOR SHOULDER ABDUCTION, FLEXION, AND EXTENSION.

ENABLE TRUNK ROTATION, LATERAL FLEXION, AND HELP MAINTAIN CORE STABILITY.

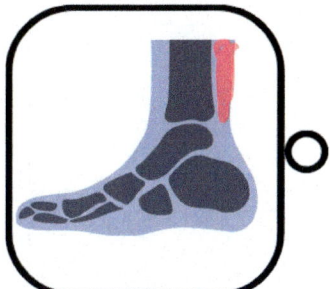

RESPONSIBLE FOR SHOULDER ADDUCTION AND FLEXION, AND PLAY A ROLE IN CHEST MOVEMENTS.

CONNECT THE CALF MUSCLES (GASTROCNEMIUS AND SOLEUS) TO THE HEEL BONE (CALCANEUS) AND ENABLE PLANTARFLEXION OF THE FOOT.

THE MUSCULAR SYSTEM

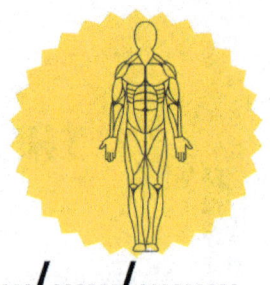

Name:……………………………… Date:……/……/………

MUSCLE DISEASES:

MUSCLE DISEASES	SYMPTOMS	TREATMENTS
MUSCULAR DYSTROPHY		
MYASTHENIA GRAVIS		
AMYOTROPHIC LATERAL SCLEROSIS		
POLYMYOSITIS AND DERMATOMYOSITIS		
FIBROMYALGIA		

THE MUSCULAR SYSTEM

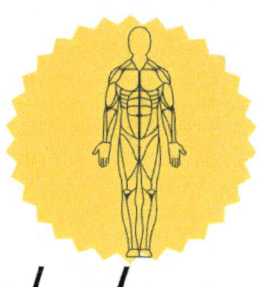

Name:............................... Date:....../....../........

MUSCLE CATEGORY:

MUSCLE CATEGORY	LOCATION	CONTROL
SKELETAL MUSCLES		
SMOOTH MUSCLES		
CARDIAC MUSCLE		

THE MUSCULAR SYSTEM

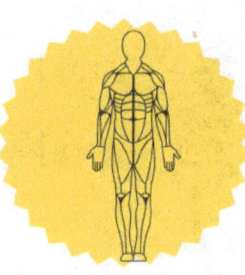

Describing How Muscles Work:

Draw a picture of the upper and lower arm, including the bones and muscles.

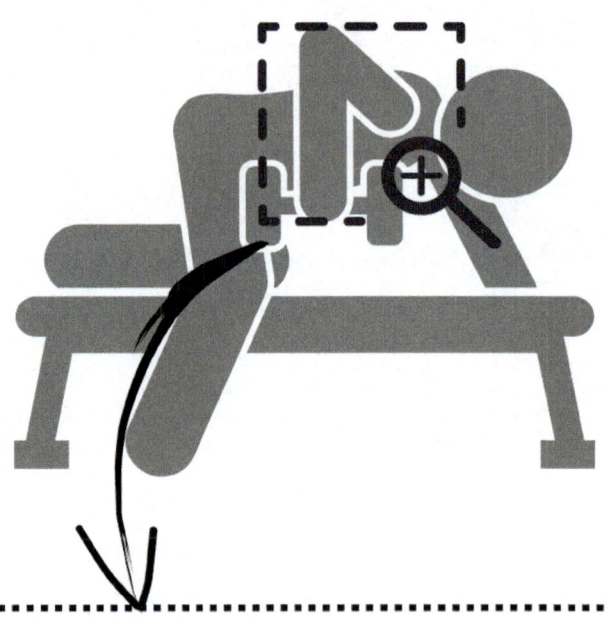

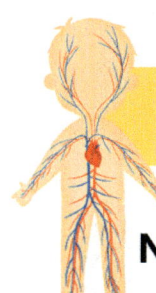

THE CIRCULATORY SYSTEM

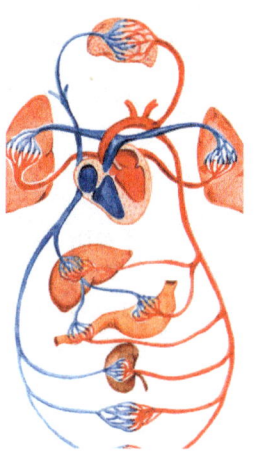

Name:............................... Date:....../....../........

what is the Circulatory System
_____
_____
_____
_____
_____

why is it important
_____
_____
_____
_____
_____
_____

the heart
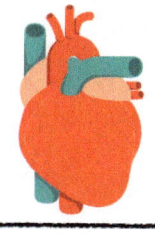
_____
_____
_____
_____
_____
_____

blood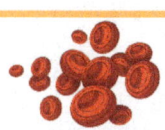
_____
_____
_____

oxygen
_____
_____
_____

THE CIRCULATORY SYSTEM
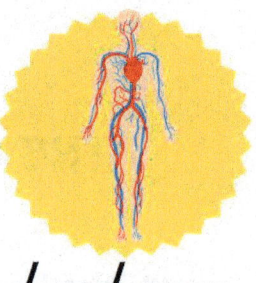

Name:............................... Date:....../....../.........

LABEL THE PARTS BELOW:

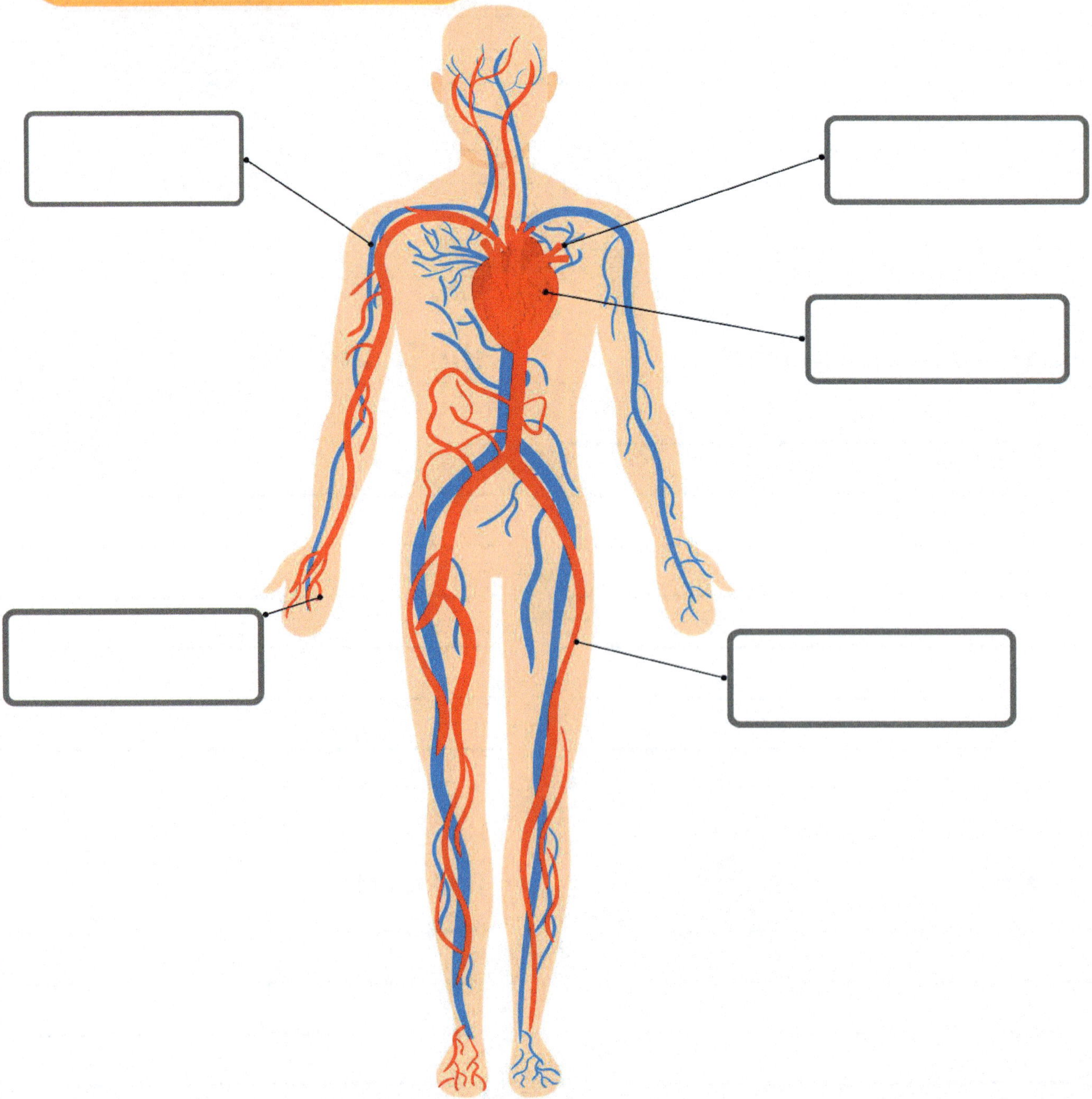

20

THE CIRCULATORY SYSTEM

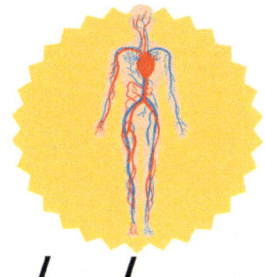

Name:................................ Date:....../....../........

Label the parts below:

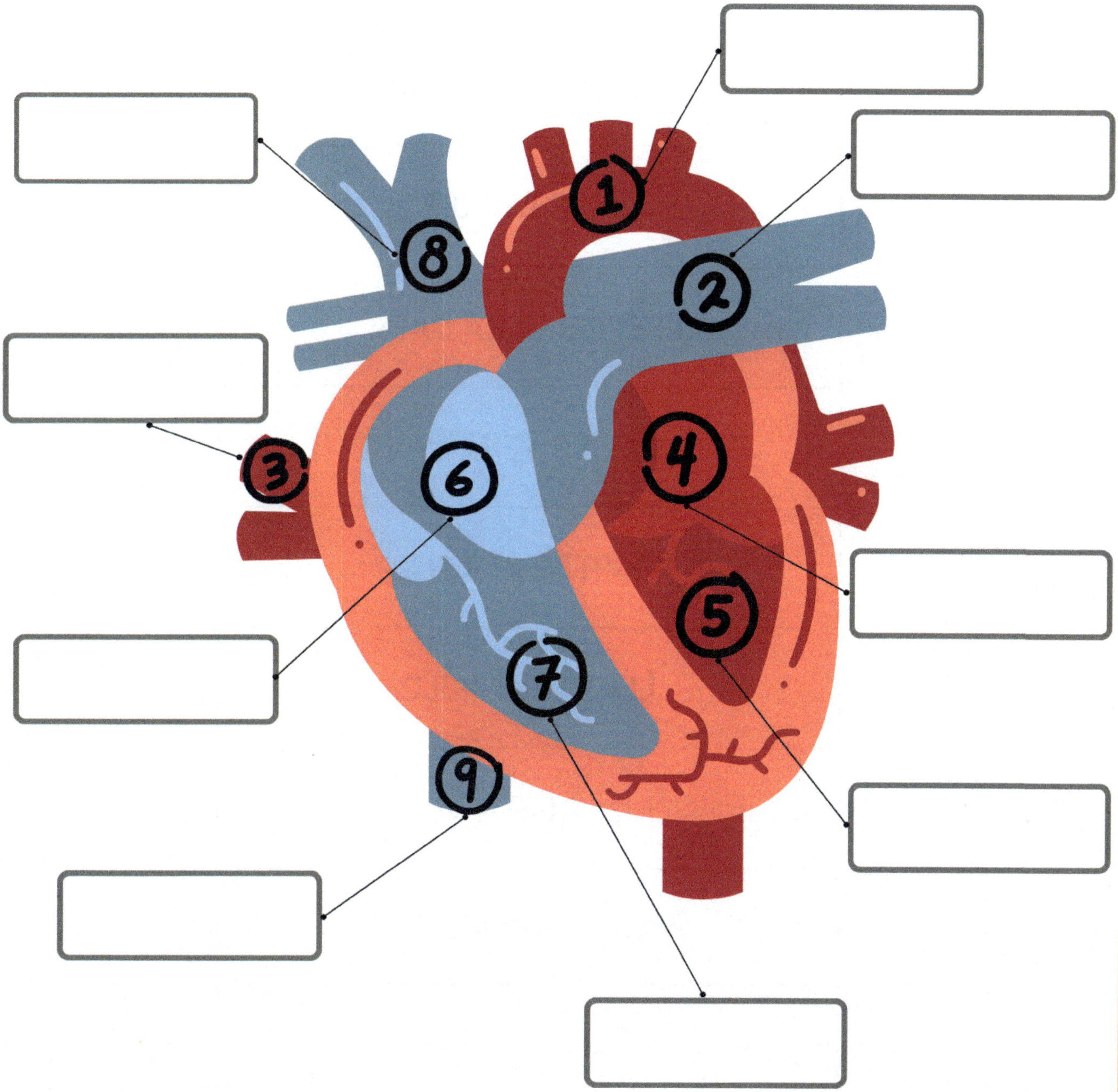

21

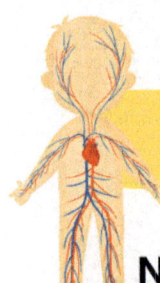
THE CIRCULATORY SYSTEM
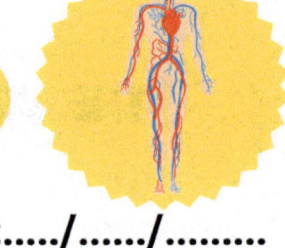

Name:............................... Date:....../....../.........

Parts of the heart

Pulmonary vein
Right atrium
Inferior vena cava
Superior vena cava
Right ventricle
Left ventricle
Aorta
Pulmonary artery
Left atrium

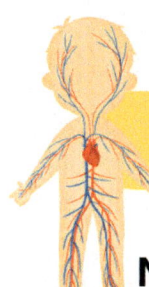
THE CIRCULATORY SYSTEM
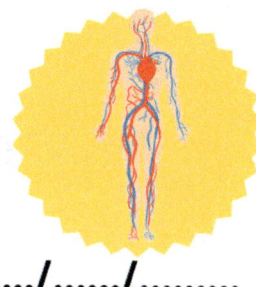

Name:............................... Date:....../....../.........

Functions:

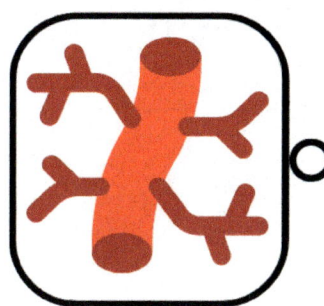

THE CENTRAL ORGAN OF THE CARDIOVASCULAR SYSTEM. IT IS A MUSCULAR PUMP THAT CONTRACTS RHYTHMICALLY TO CIRCULATE BLOOD THROUGHOUT THE BODY.

RETURN DEOXYGENATED BLOOD TO THE HEART.

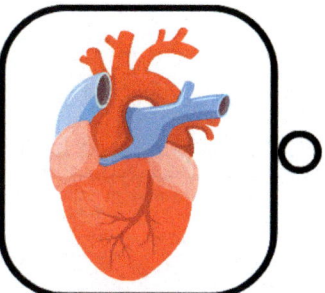

FACILITATE THE EXCHANGE OF NUTRIENTS AND OXYGEN WITH TISSUES.

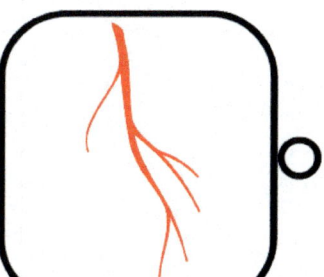

CARRY OXYGENATED BLOOD AWAY FROM THE HEART.

THE CIRCULATORY SYSTEM

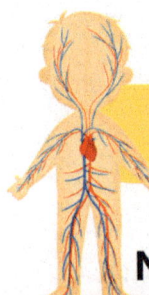

Name:................................ Date:....../....../..........

Circulatory System Diseases:

DISEASES	SYMPTOMS	TREATMENTS
CORONARY ARTERY DISEASE		
HYPERTENSION		
STROKE		
CONGESTIVE HEART FAILURE		
PERIPHERAL ARTERY DISEASE		

THE CIRCULATORY SYSTEM

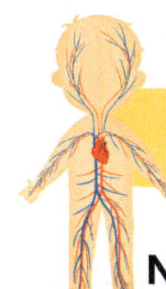

Name:............................ Date:...../...../.........

Fill in the blanks and answer the questions based on your knowledge of the cardiovascular system.

1. The _____ is a muscular organ responsible for pumping blood throughout the body.
2. Blood vessels that carry oxygenated blood away from the heart are called _____.
3. The _____ is the largest artery in the body and carries oxygenated blood from the heart to the rest of the body.
4. _____ are tiny blood vessels where the exchange of oxygen and nutrients for waste products occurs in tissues.
5. The _____ is a thin-walled, oxygen-poor chamber of the heart that receives blood from the body.
6. The _____ valve prevents the backflow of blood from the left ventricle into the left atrium.
7. The _____ is a large, oxygen-rich chamber of the heart that pumps blood into the systemic circulation.
8. _____ is a condition characterized by the buildup of fatty deposits in the arteries, leading to reduced blood flow.

Bank of Words

- Atherosclerosis
- Arteries
- Capillaries
- Aorta
- Heart
- Right atrium
- Left ventricle
- Mitral valve

THE RESPIRATORY SYSTEM

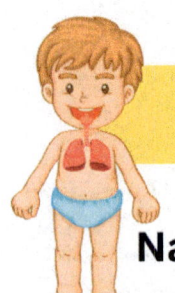

Name:............................... Date:....../....../.........

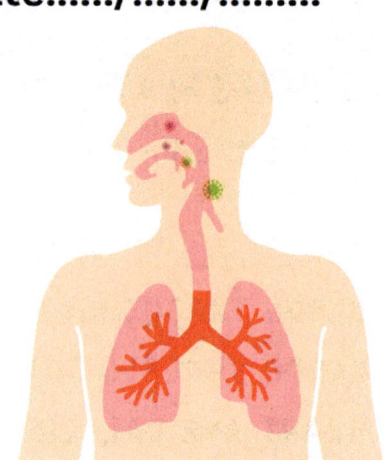

what is the Respiratory System
_____
_____
_____
_____
_____
_____

why is it important
_____
_____
_____
_____
_____
_____

Lungs
_____
_____
_____
_____
_____
_____

Throat
_____
_____
_____
_____

oxygen
_____
_____
_____
_____

THE RESPIRATORY SYSTEM

Name:............................... Date:....../....../.........

Label the parts below:

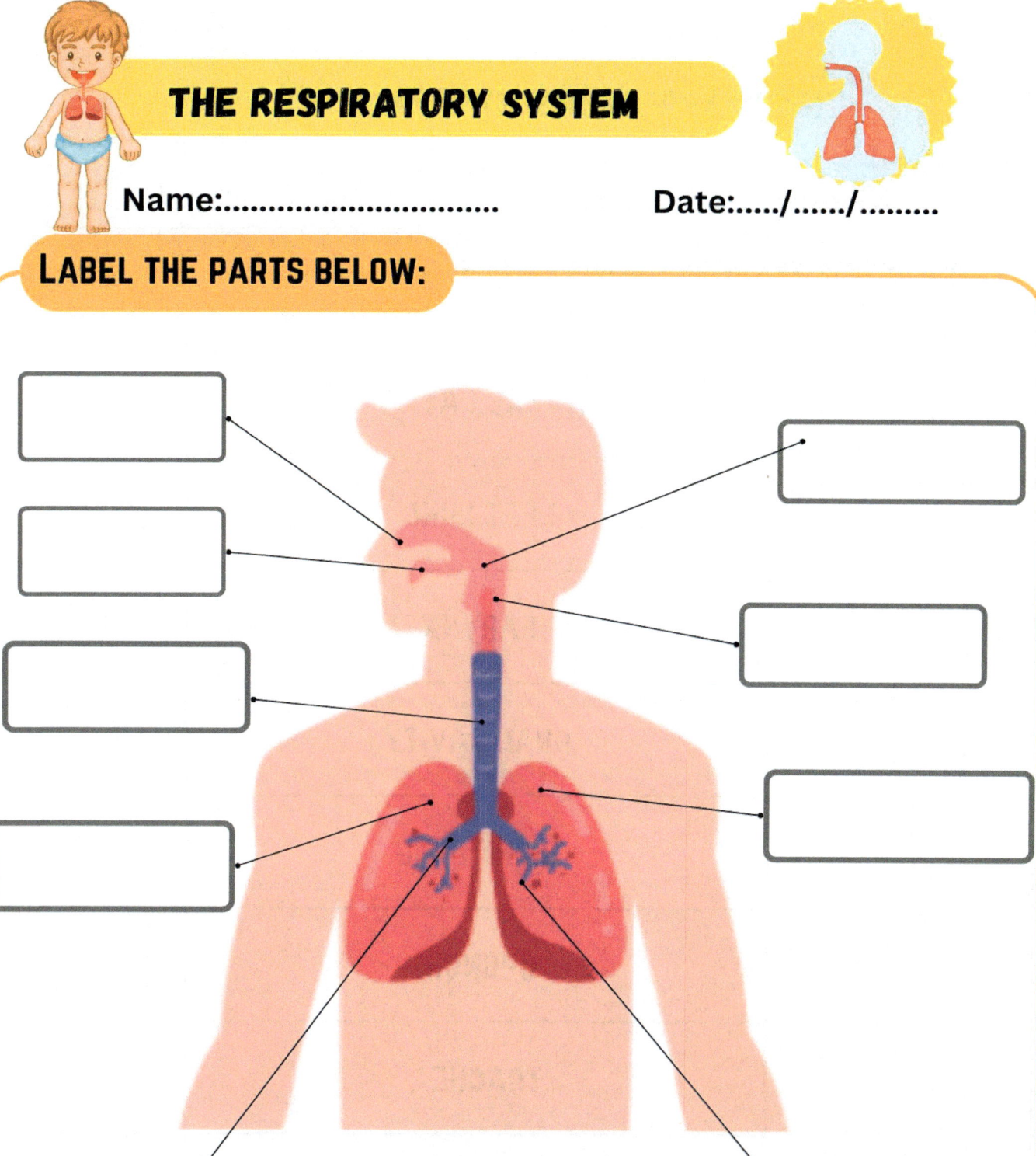

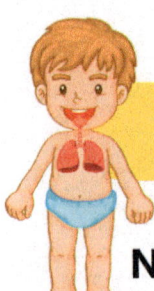

THE RESPIRATORY SYSTEM

Name:............................... Date:....../....../.........

Parts of the Respiratory System

NASAL CAVITY
LEFT LUNG
LARYNX
ORAL CAVITY
RIGHT LUNG
BRONCHI
TRACHEA
BRONCHIOLES
PHARYNX

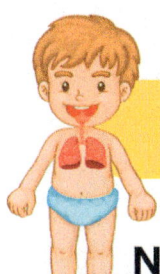

THE RESPIRATORY SYSTEM

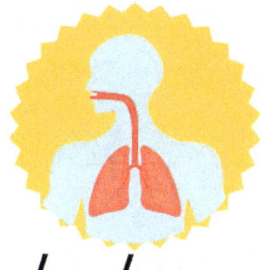

Name:............................ Date:....../....../.........

CONNECT EACH PARTS TO THEIR FUNCTION

nasal cavity   FACILITATE GAS EXCHANGE FOR RESPIRATION.

lungs   FILTERS, WARMS, AND HUMIDIFIES INHALED AIR.

larynx   INITIATES DIGESTION THROUGH MASTICATION AND SALIVATION.

oral cavity   PRODUCES SOUND AND PROTECTS THE AIRWAY.

THE RESPIRATORY SYSTEM

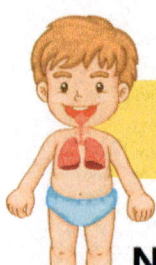
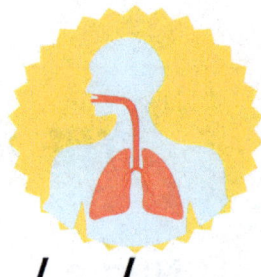

Name:........................... Date:....../....../........

Connect each parts to their function

bronchi ○———○ PROVIDING STRUCTURAL SUPPORT

trachea ○———○ FACILITATING AIR PASSAGE

pharynx ○———○ AIDING IN BOTH RESPIRATION AND DIGESTION

THE RESPIRATORY SYSTEM

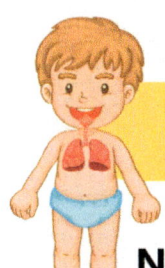

Name:................................ Date:....../....../.........

Circulatory System Diseases:

DISEASES	SYMPTOMS	TREATMENTS
CORONAVIRUS DISEASE 2019		
INFLUENZA		
ASTHMA		
CHRONIC OBSTRUCTIVE PULMONARY		
TUBERCULOSIS		

THE RESPIRATORY SYSTEM

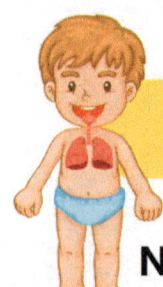
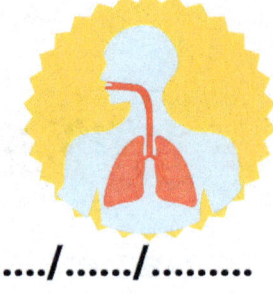

Name:............................ Date:....../....../.........

Choose the correct answer:

1- What is the primary function of the respiratory system?
- A) DIGESTION
- B) OXYGEN TRANSPORT
- C) BLOOD CIRCULATION
- D) MUSCLE MOVEMENT

2- Which of the following is not part of the lower respiratory tract?
- A) TRACHEA
- B) LARYNX
- C) BRONCHI
- D) PHARYNX

3- Where does gas exchange between oxygen and carbon dioxide occur in the lungs?
- A) TRACHEA
- B) BRONCHIOLES
- C) ALVEOLI
- D) DIAPHRAGM

4- What is the term for the process of breathing out air from the lungs?
- A) INHALATION
- B) EXHALATION
- C) RESPIRATION
- D) ASPIRATION

5- Which of the following is a common respiratory disorder characterized by narrowing of the airways and difficulty breathing?
- A) PNEUMONIA
- B) BRONCHITIS
- C) ASTHMA
- D) TUBERCULOSIS

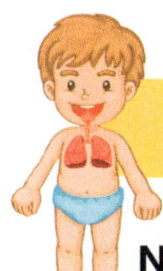

THE RESPIRATORY SYSTEM

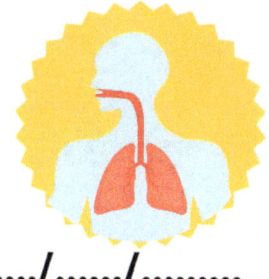

Name:............................. Date:....../....../..........

CHOOSE THE CORRECT ANSWER:

6- What is the function of the epiglottis in the respiratory system?

- A REGULATING BLOOD FLOW
- B PRODUCING MUCUS
- C EXCHANGING GASES
- D PREVENTING FOOD FROM ENTERING THE AIRWAY

7- What muscle plays a crucial role in the process of inhalation?

- A DIAPHRAGM
- B BICEPS
- C QUADRICEPS
- D PECTORALIS MAJOR

8- Which gas is primarily responsible for stimulating the body's respiratory rate and depth?

- A OXYGEN (O2)
- B CARBON DIOXIDE (CO2)
- C NITROGEN (N2)
- D HYDROGEN (H2)

9- Which structure separates the nasal and oral cavities from the larynx and esophagus, ensuring that food and liquids go down the digestive system and not into the respiratory system?

- A UVULA
- B TONSILS
- C EPIGLOTTIS
- D TRACHEA

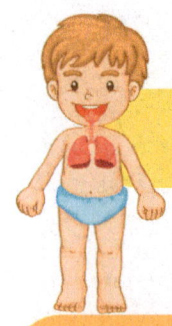 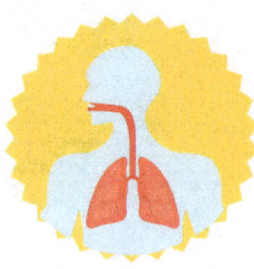

THE RESPIRATORY SYSTEM

ANSWERS:

1- Oxygen transport

2- Pharynx

3- Alveoli

4- Exhalation

5- Asthma

6- Preventing food from entering the airway

7- Diaphragm

8- Carbon dioxide (CO_2)

9- Epiglottis

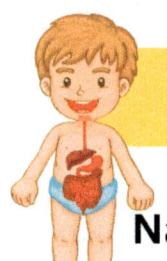
THE DIGESTIVE SYSTEM
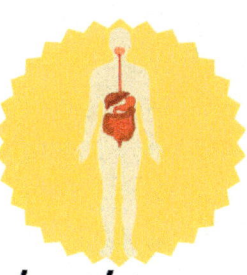

Name:............................... Date:....../....../..........

what is the Digestive System
_____
_____
_____
_____
_____

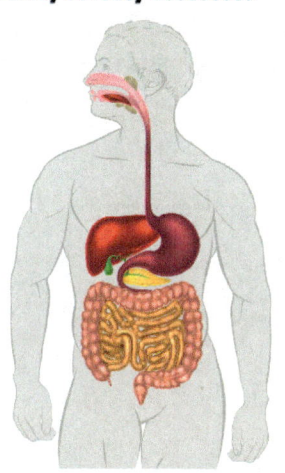

why is it important
_____
_____
_____
_____
_____
_____

Stomach
_____
_____
_____
_____
_____
_____

Small Intestine
_____
_____
_____
_____

Liver
_____
_____
_____
_____

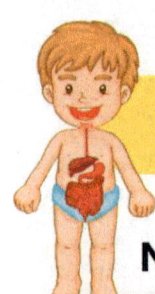

THE DIGESTIVE SYSTEM

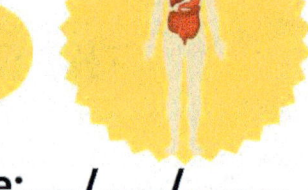

Name:............................... Date:....../....../.........

Label the parts below:

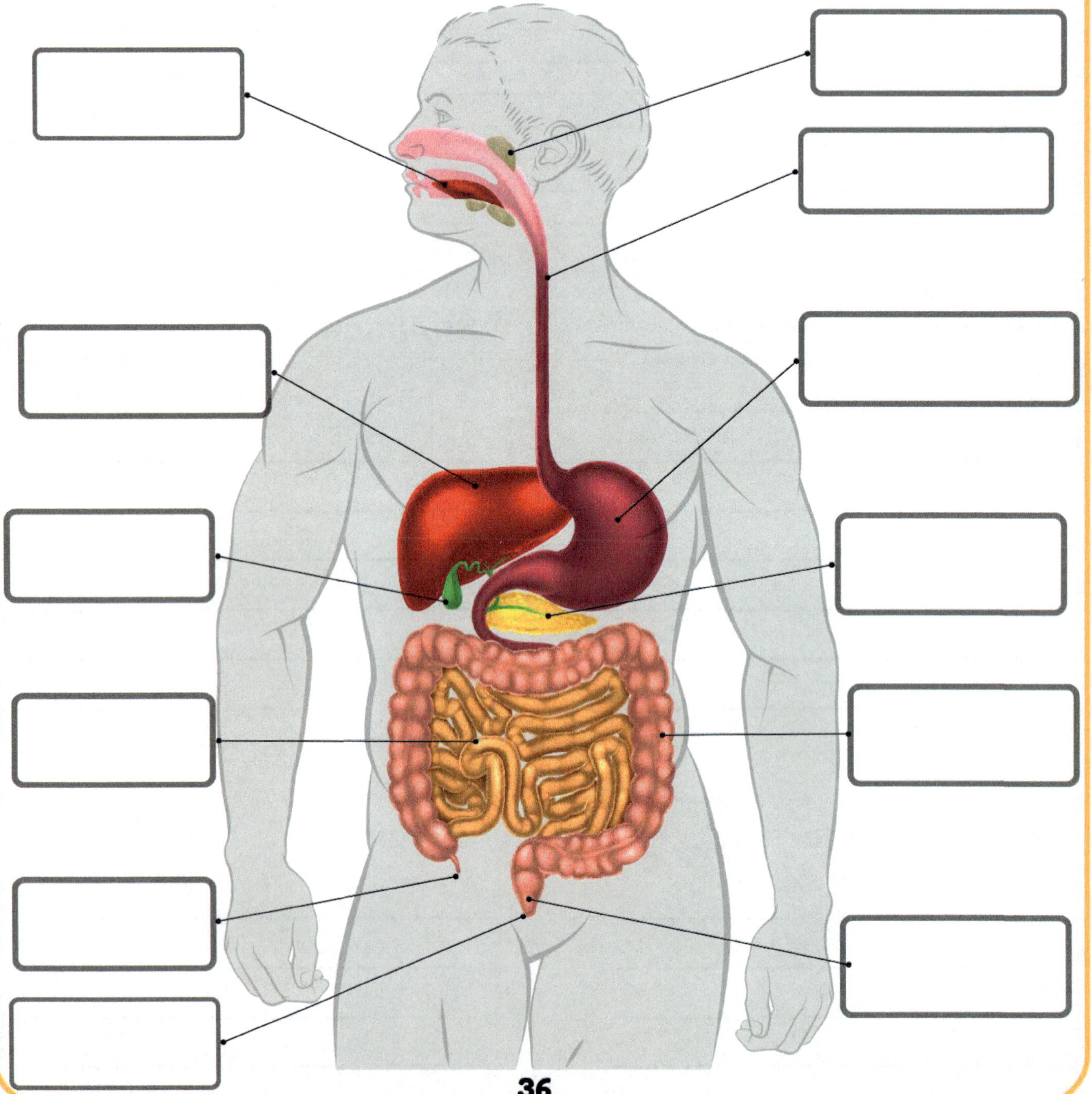

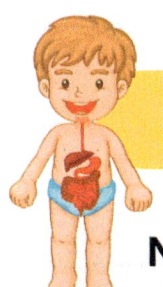

THE DIGESTIVE SYSTEM

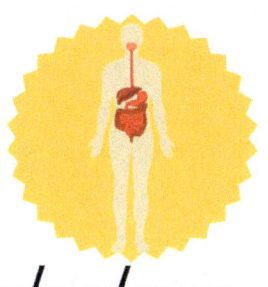

Name:............................ Date:....../....../.........

Parts of the Digestive System

LIVER	STOMACH
SMALL INTESTINE	MOUTH
SALIVARY GLADES	APPENDIX
LARGE INTESTINE	ANUS
RECTUM	ESOPHAGUS
GALLBLADDER	PANCREAS

THE DIGESTIVE SYSTEM

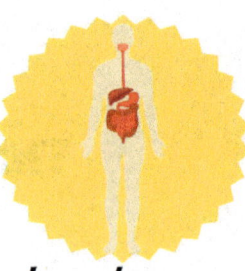

Name:............................... Date:....../....../..........

Functions:

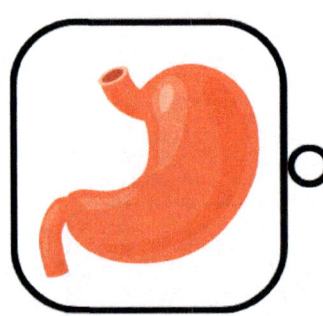

PROPELS CHEWED FOOD FROM THE MOUTH TO THE STOMACH VIA PERISTALTIC CONTRACTIONS.

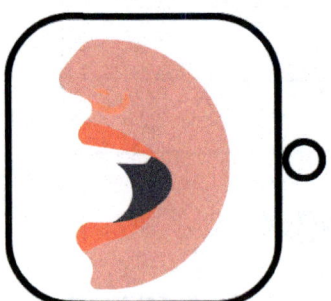

BEGINS MECHANICAL AND ENZYMATIC DIGESTION OF FOOD THROUGH CHEWING AND SALIVARY ENZYME ACTION.

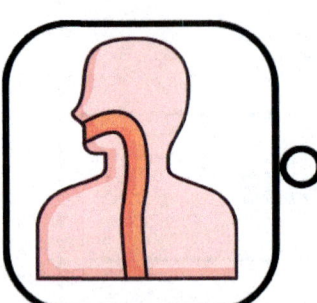

OMPLETES DIGESTION AND ABSORBS NUTRIENTS WITH THE HELP OF ENZYMES, BILE, AND SPECIALIZED CELLS IN ITS LINING.

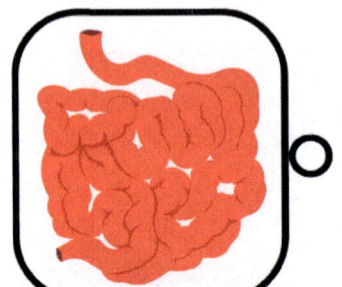

STORES, MIXES, AND PARTIALLY DIGESTS FOOD USING GASTRIC JUICES, CREATING CHYME.

THE DIGESTIVE SYSTEM

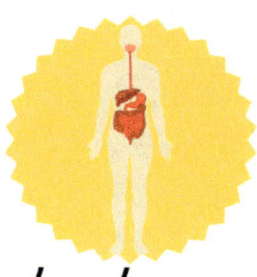

Name:............................. Date:....../....../.........

FUNCTIONS:

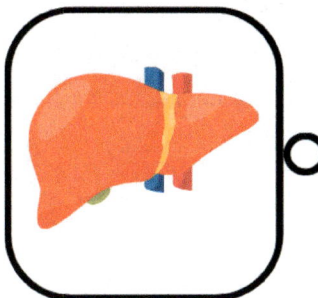

PRODUCES DIGESTIVE ENZYMES AND REGULATES BLOOD SUGAR WITH INSULIN AND GLUCAGON.

DETOXIFIES BLOOD, PRODUCES BILE FOR FAT DIGESTION, AND STORES NUTRIENTS.

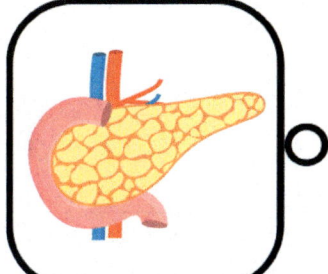

STORES AND RELEASES BILE TO AID IN FAT DIGESTION.

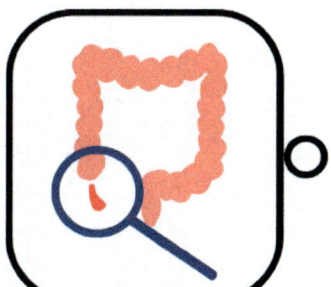

PLAY A ROLE IN THE IMMUNE SYSTEM AND GUT HEALTH.

THE DIGESTIVE SYSTEM

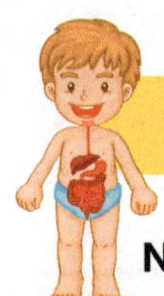

Name:............................ Date:....../....../.........

Digestive System Diseases:

DISEASES	SYMPTOMS	TREATMENTS
GASTROESOPHAGEAL REFLUX DISEASE		
IRRITABLE BOWEL SYNDROME		
INFLAMMATORY BOWEL DISEASE		
CELIAC DISEASE		
PANCREATITIS		

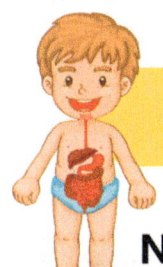
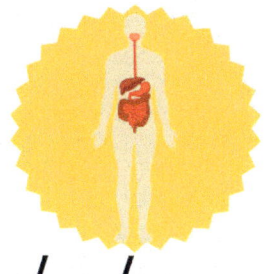

THE DIGESTIVE SYSTEM

Name:................................ Date:....../....../.........

CHOOSE THE CORRECT ANSWER:

1- What is the primary function of the small intestine?

- A) ABSORB WATER AND ELECTROLYTES
- B) STORE FOOD TEMPORARILY
- C) DIGEST PROTEINS AND CARBOHYDRATES
- D) ELIMINATE WASTE PRODUCTS

2- Which organ produces and stores bile?

- A) STOMACH
- B) LIVER
- C) GALLBLADDER
- D) PANCREAS

3- What is the primary role of the pancreas in digestion?

- A) PRODUCING BILE
- B) ABSORBING NUTRIENTS
- C) REGULATING BLOOD SUGAR
- D) PRODUCING DIGESTIVE ENZYMES

4- Which of the following is NOT a part of the large intestine?

- A) COLON
- B) RECTUM
- C) DUODENUM
- D) CECUM

5- What is the function of the appendix?

- A) DIGESTING CARBOHYDRATES
- B) STORING EXCESS BILE
- C) AIDING IN IMMUNE SYSTEM FUNCTION
- D) ABSORBING NUTRIENTS

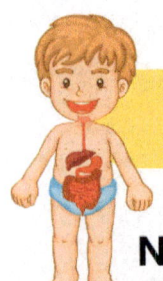
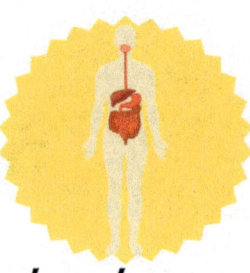

THE DIGESTIVE SYSTEM

Name:............................ Date:....../....../........

Choose the correct answer:

6- What enzyme found in saliva begins the digestion of starches in the mouth?

- A LIPASE
- B PROTEASE
- C AMYLASE
- D MALTASE

7- The process of moving food through the esophagus to the stomach through rhythmic muscle contractions is called:

- A PERISTALSIS
- B DIGESTION
- C EMULSIFICATION
- D FERMENTATION

8- Where does most of the absorption of nutrients take place in the digestive system?

- A STOMACH
- B SMALL INTESTINE
- C LARGE INTESTINE
- D GALLBLADDER

9- Which digestive organ is responsible for breaking down proteins with the help of gastric juices?

- A LIVER
- B GALLBLADDER
- C STOMACH
- D PANCREAS

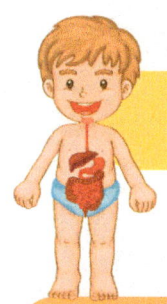
THE DIGESTIVE SYSTEM
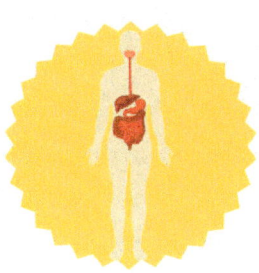

ANSWERS:

1-Digest proteins and carbohydrates

2-Gallbladder

3-Producing digestive enzymes

4-Duodenum

5-Aiding in immune system function

6-Amylase

7-Peristalsis

8-Small intestine

9-Stomach

THE NERVOUS SYSTEM

Name:............................... Date:....../....../.........

what is the Nervous System
_____
_____
_____
_____
_____
_____

why is it important
_____
_____
_____
_____
_____
_____

Brain
_____
_____
_____
_____
_____
_____

Spinal Cord
_____
_____
_____
_____

Neurons
_____
_____
_____
_____

THE NERVOUS SYSTEM

Name:............................... Date:....../....../.........

Label the parts below:

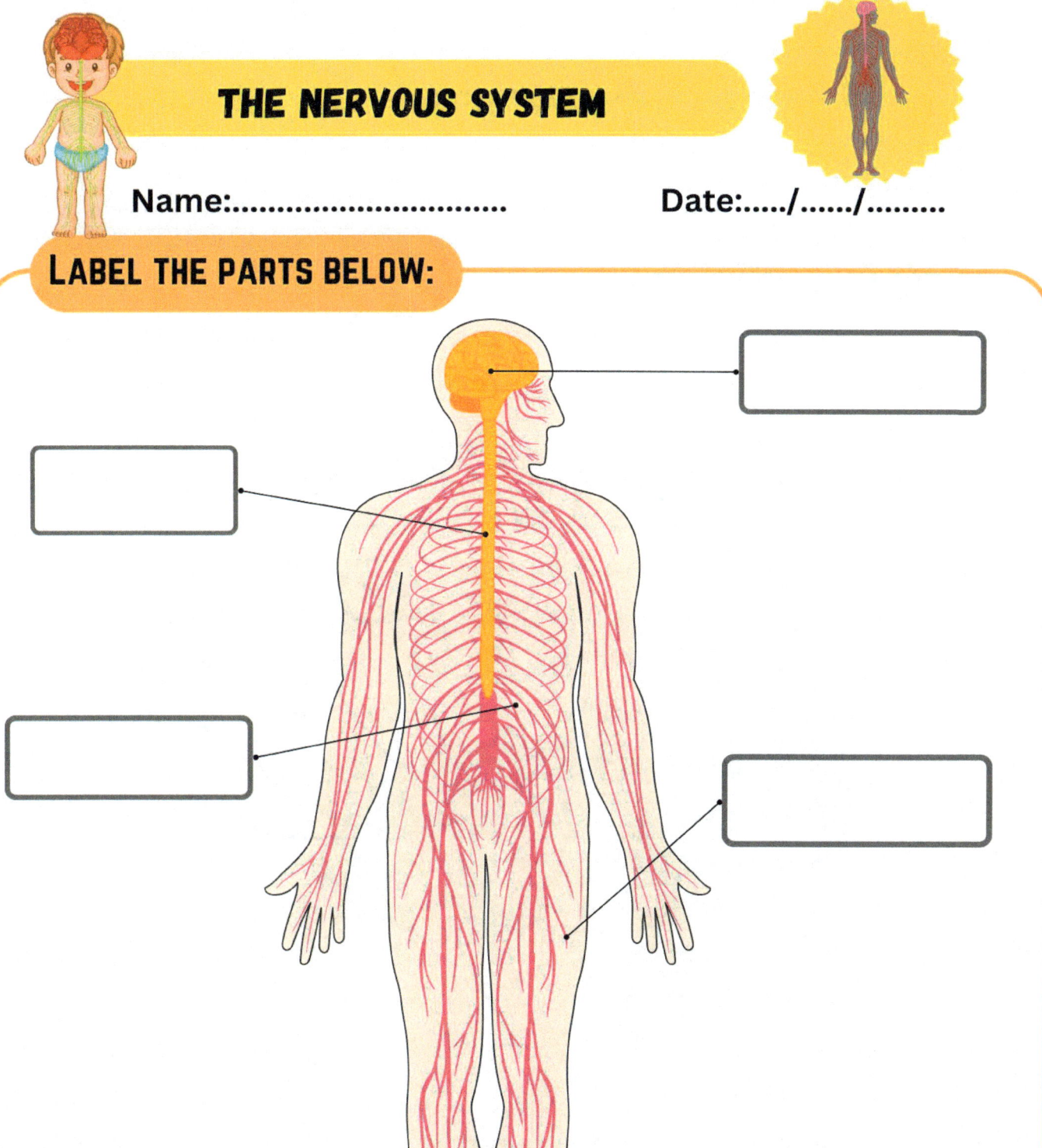

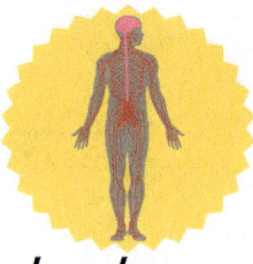

THE NERVOUS SYSTEM

Name:............................   Date:....../....../........

Parts of the brain

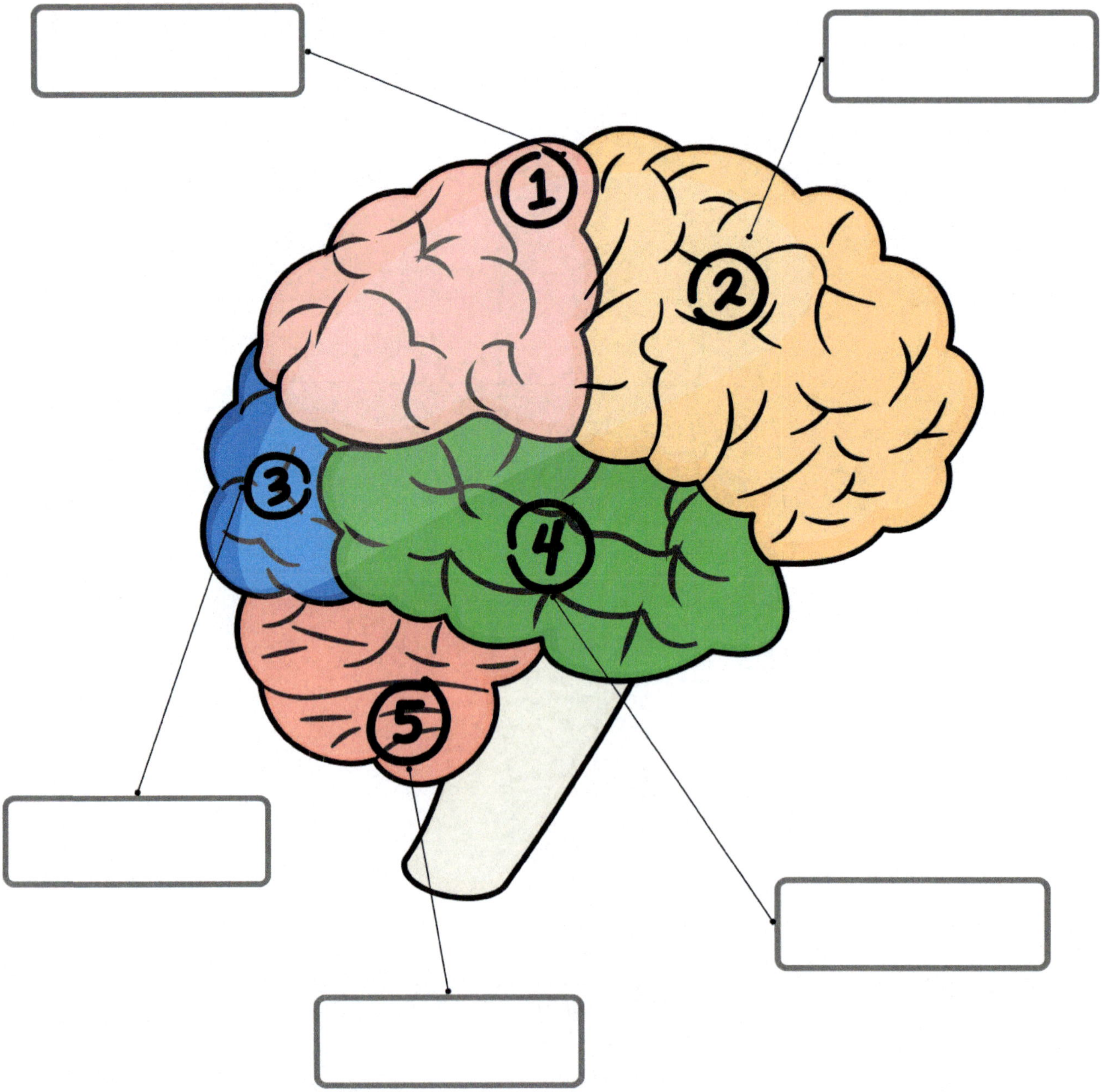

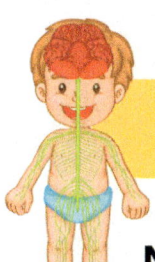
THE NERVOUS SYSTEM
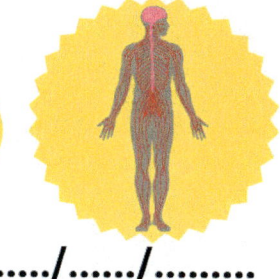

Name:................................ Date:....../....../.........

Parts of the brain

AUTONOMIC NERVES
Brain
PERIPHERAL NERVES
Spinal Cord
Parietal lobe
Frontal lobe
Temporal lobe
Occipital lobe
Cerebellum

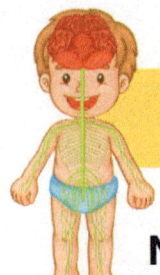
THE NERVOUS SYSTEM
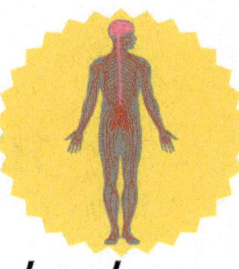

Name:............................   Date:....../....../..........

Functions:

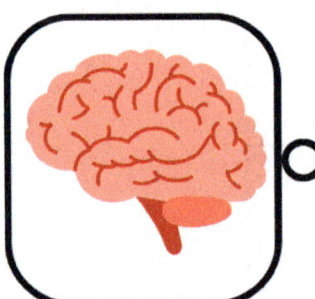
SERVES AS A COMMUNICATION PATHWAY BETWEEN THE BRAIN AND THE BODY, RELAYING SENSORY INFORMATION AND COORDINATING MOTOR RESPONSES, INCLUDING REFLEXES.

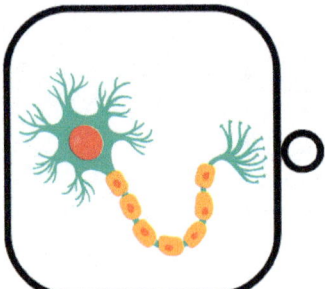
RANSMIT SIGNALS BETWEEN THE CENTRAL NERVOUS SYSTEM AND THE BODY'S EXTREMITIES, ENABLING SENSORY INPUT AND MOTOR OUTPUT FOR MOVEMENT AND SENSATION.

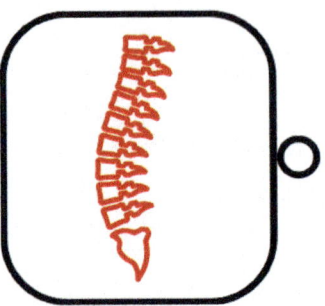
IS THE CENTRAL CONTROL CENTER OF THE NERVOUS SYSTEM, RESPONSIBLE FOR PROCESSING INFORMATION, COORDINATING BODY FUNCTIONS, AND GENERATING THOUGHTS AND EMOTIONS.

TRANSMIT ELECTRICAL SIGNALS TO CONVEY INFORMATION THROUGHOUT THE NERVOUS SYSTEM, FACILITATING SENSORY PERCEPTION, MOTOR CONTROL, AND COGNITIVE PROCESSES.

THE NERVOUS SYSTEM

Name:............................... Date:....../....../........

The Nervous System Diseases:

DISEASES	SYMPTOMS	TREATMENTS
ALZHEIMER'S DISEASE		
PARKINSON'S DISEASE		
MULTIPLE SCLEROSIS		
AMYOTROPHIC LATERAL SCLEROSIS		
EPILEPSY		

THE NERVOUS SYSTEM

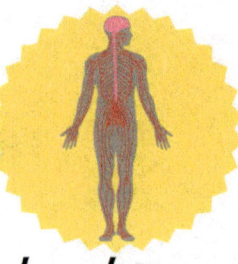

Name:............................ Date:....../....../........

Choose the correct answer:

1- What is the primary function of the nervous system?

| A | DIGESTION | B | COMMUNICATION AND CONTROL |
| C | RESPIRATION | D | CIRCULATION |

2- Which part of the nervous system is responsible for involuntary actions like heartbeat and digestion?

| A | CENTRAL NERVOUS SYSTEM | B | PERIPHERAL NERVOUS SYSTEM |
| C | AUTONOMIC NERVOUS SYSTEM | D | SOMATIC NERVOUS SYSTEM |

3- Which of the following is the largest part of the brain and responsible for higher-order thinking and decision-making?

| A | CEREBELLUM | B | MEDULLA OBLONGATA |
| C | CEREBRUM | D | THALAMUS |

4- Which neurotransmitter is commonly associated with feelings of pleasure and reward?

| A | SEROTONIN | B | DOPAMINE |
| C | GABA | D | ACETYLCHOLINE |

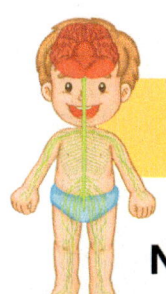
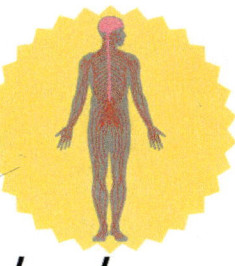

THE NERVOUS SYSTEM

Name:............................ Date:...../....../..........

Choose the correct answer:

5- Which part of a neuron receives signals from other neurons or sensory receptors?

| A | AXON | B | DENDRITE |
| C | SYNAPSE | D | MYELIN SHEATH |

6- What is the main function of the spinal cord in the nervous system?

| A | PROCESSING SENSORY INFORMATION | B | THINKING AND DECISION-MAKING |
| C | TRANSMITTING SIGNALS BETWEEN THE BRAIN AND THE REST OF THE BODY | D | FILTERING BLOOD |

7- Which of the following is NOT one of the main divisions of the autonomic nervous system?

| A | SYMPATHETIC NERVOUS SYSTEM | B | PARASYMPATHETIC NERVOUS SYSTEM |
| C | ENTERIC NERVOUS SYSTEM | D | SOMATIC NERVOUS SYSTEM |

8- Which disorder is characterized by the loss of myelin sheath in the central nervous system, leading to impaired communication between nerve cells?

| A | PARKINSON'S DISEASE | B | ALZHEIMER'S DISEASE |
| C | MULTIPLE SCLEROSIS | D | EPILEPSY |

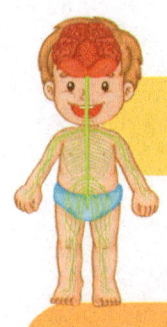

THE NERVOUS SYSTEM

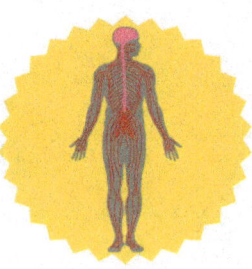

ANSWERS:

1- Communication and control

2- Autonomic nervous system

3- Cerebrum

4- Dopamine

5- Dendrite

6- Transmitting signals between the brain and the rest of the body

7- Somatic nervous system

8- Multiple sclerosis

THE ENDOCRINE SYSTEM

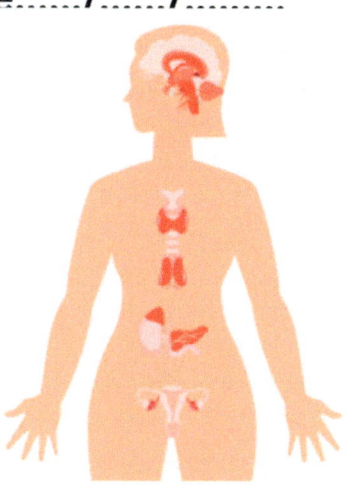

Name:........................... Date:....../....../......

what is the Endocrine System
_____
_____
_____
_____
_____
_____

why is it important
_____
_____
_____
_____
_____
_____
_____

pancreas
_____
_____
_____
_____
_____
_____
_____

Pineal gland
_____
_____
_____
_____

thyroid
_____
_____
_____
_____

THE ENDOCRINE SYSTEM

Name:............................ Date:....../....../........

Label the parts below:

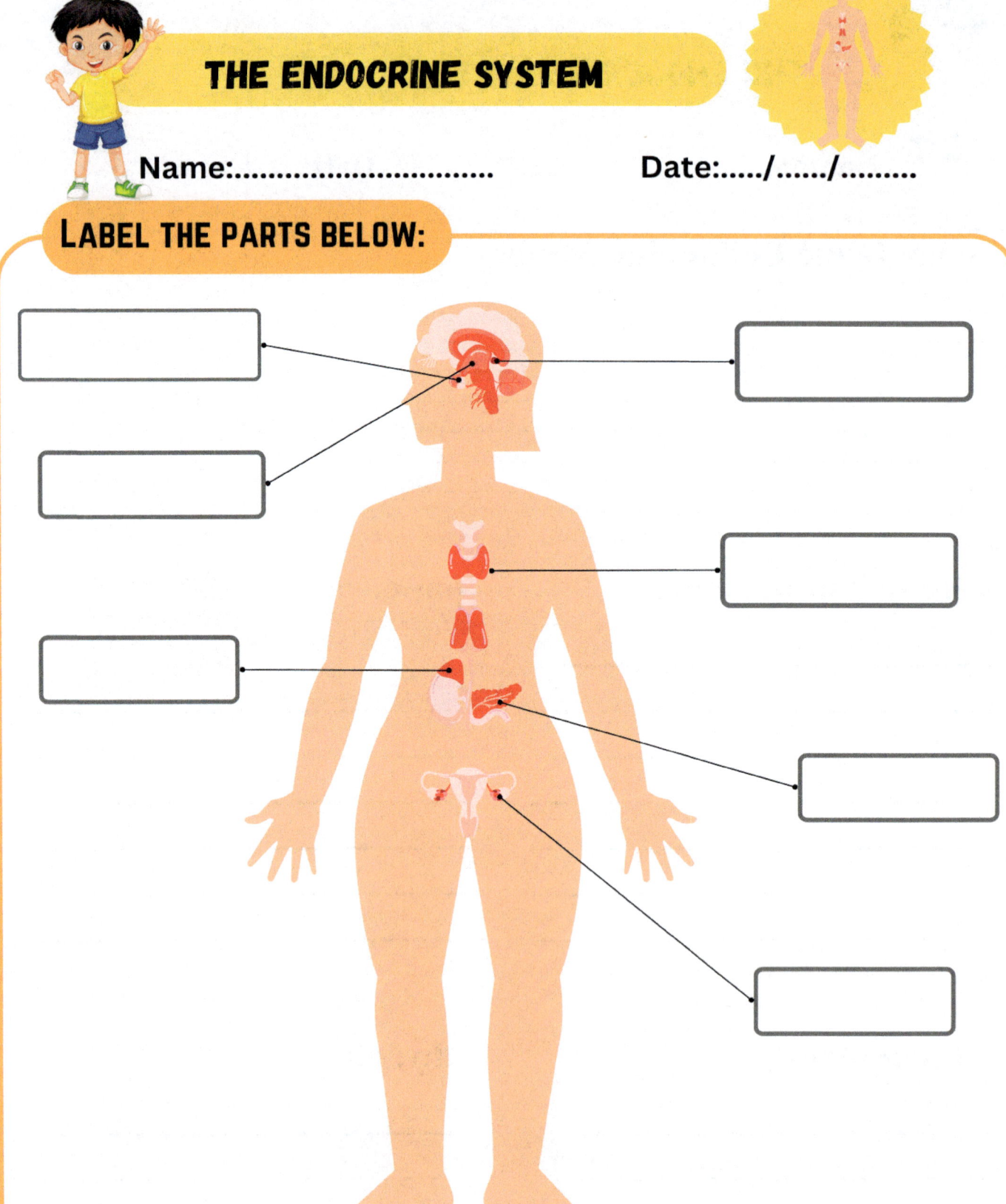

THE ENDOCRINE SYSTEM

Name:............................. Date:....../....../..........

Parts of the Endocrine System

THYROID
PINEAL GLAND
HYPOTHALAMUS
ADRENAL GLAND
PANCREAS
OVARY
PITUITARY GLAND

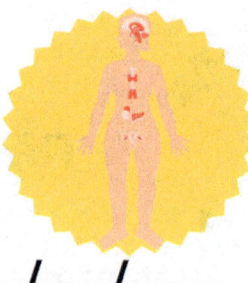

THE ENDOCRINE SYSTEM

Name:............................... Date:....../....../..........

Functions:

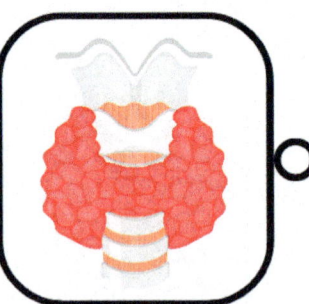

REGULATES BLOOD SUGAR LEVELS BY PRODUCING INSULIN (LOWERS BLOOD SUGAR) AND GLUCAGON (RAISES BLOOD SUGAR).

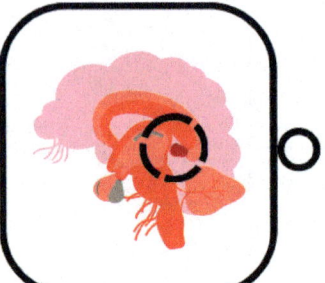

REGULATES METABOLISM BY PRODUCING HORMONES (T3 AND T4) THAT INFLUENCE ENERGY PRODUCTION AND BODY TEMPERATURE.

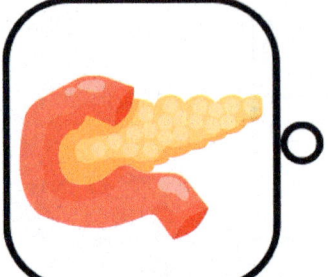

PRODUCE HORMONES (ESTROGEN AND PROGESTERONE) THAT CONTROL FEMALE REPRODUCTIVE DEVELOPMENT AND THE MENSTRUAL CYCLE.

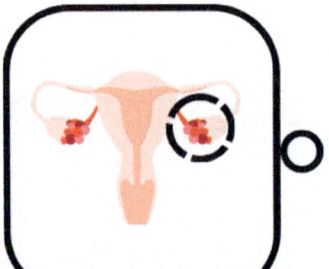

PRODUCES MELATONIN, WHICH HELPS REGULATE THE SLEEP-WAKE CYCLE AND CIRCADIAN RHYTHMS.

THE ENDOCRINE SYSTEM

Name:.............................. Date:....../....../.........

The Endocrine System Diseases:

DISEASES	SYMPTOMS	TREATMENTS
DIABETES MELLITUS		
HYPERTHYROIDISM		
CUSHING'S SYNDROME		
ADDISON'S DISEASE		
ACROMEGALY		

THE ENDOCRINE SYSTEM

Name:.............................. Date:....../....../..........

CHOOSE THE CORRECT ANSWER:

1- Which gland is often referred to as the "master gland" because it controls many other endocrine glands in the body?

| A | THYROID GLAND | B | PITUITARY GLAND |
| C | ADRENAL GLAND | D | PANCREAS |

2- What hormone is responsible for regulating blood sugar levels in the body?

| A | INSULIN | B | GLUCAGON |
| C | THYROXINE | D | EPINEPHRINE |

3- Which of the following hormones is produced by the adrenal glands and is often associated with the "fight or flight" response?

| A | ESTROGEN | B | PROGESTERONE |
| C | CORTISOL | D | MELATONIN |

4- The thyroid gland primarily produces which hormone that regulates metabolism?

| A | ESTROGEN | B | TESTOSTERONE |
| C | THYROXINE (T4) | D | OXYTOCIN |

THE ENDOCRINE SYSTEM

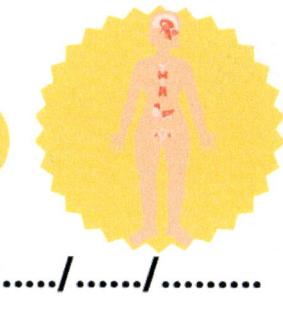

Name:............................... Date:...../...../..........

Choose the correct answer:

5- Which hormone is responsible for the development of male secondary sexual characteristics, such as facial hair and a deep voice?

- A ESTROGEN
- B PROGESTERONE
- C TESTOSTERONE
- D INSULIN

6- What is the role of the pancreas in the endocrine system?

- A PRODUCING INSULIN AND GLUCAGON
- B PRODUCING THYROID HORMONES
- C REGULATING CALCIUM LEVELS IN THE BLOOD
- D CONTROLLING STRESS RESPONSE

7- Which gland is responsible for producing melatonin, a hormone that regulates sleep-wake cycles?

- A PITUITARY GLAND
- B PINEAL GLAND
- C THYMUS GLAND
- D PARATHYROID GLAND

8- Prolactin is a hormone that plays a role in:

- A REGULATING CALCIUM LEVELS IN THE BLOOD
- B STIMULATING MILK PRODUCTION IN THE BREASTS
- C CONTROLLING BLOOD SUGAR LEVELS
- D PROMOTING THE GROWTH OF LONG BONES

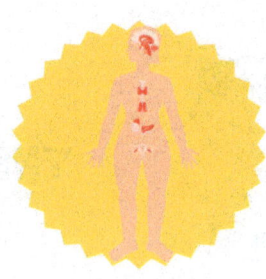

THE ENDOCRINE SYSTEM

ANSWERS:

1- Pituitary gland

2- Insulin

3- Cortisol

4- Thyroxine (T4)

5- Testosterone

6- Producing insulin and glucagon

7- Pineal gland

8- Stimulating milk production in the breasts

THE IMMUNE SYSTEM

Name:............................... Date:....../....../.........

what is the Immune System

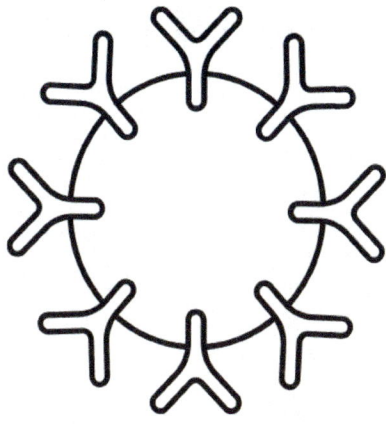

why is it important

spleen
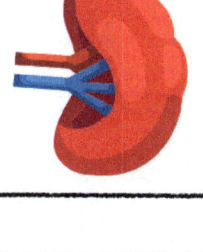

thymus

lymph nodes

THE IMMUNE SYSTEM

Name:............................... Date:....../....../.........

Label the parts below:

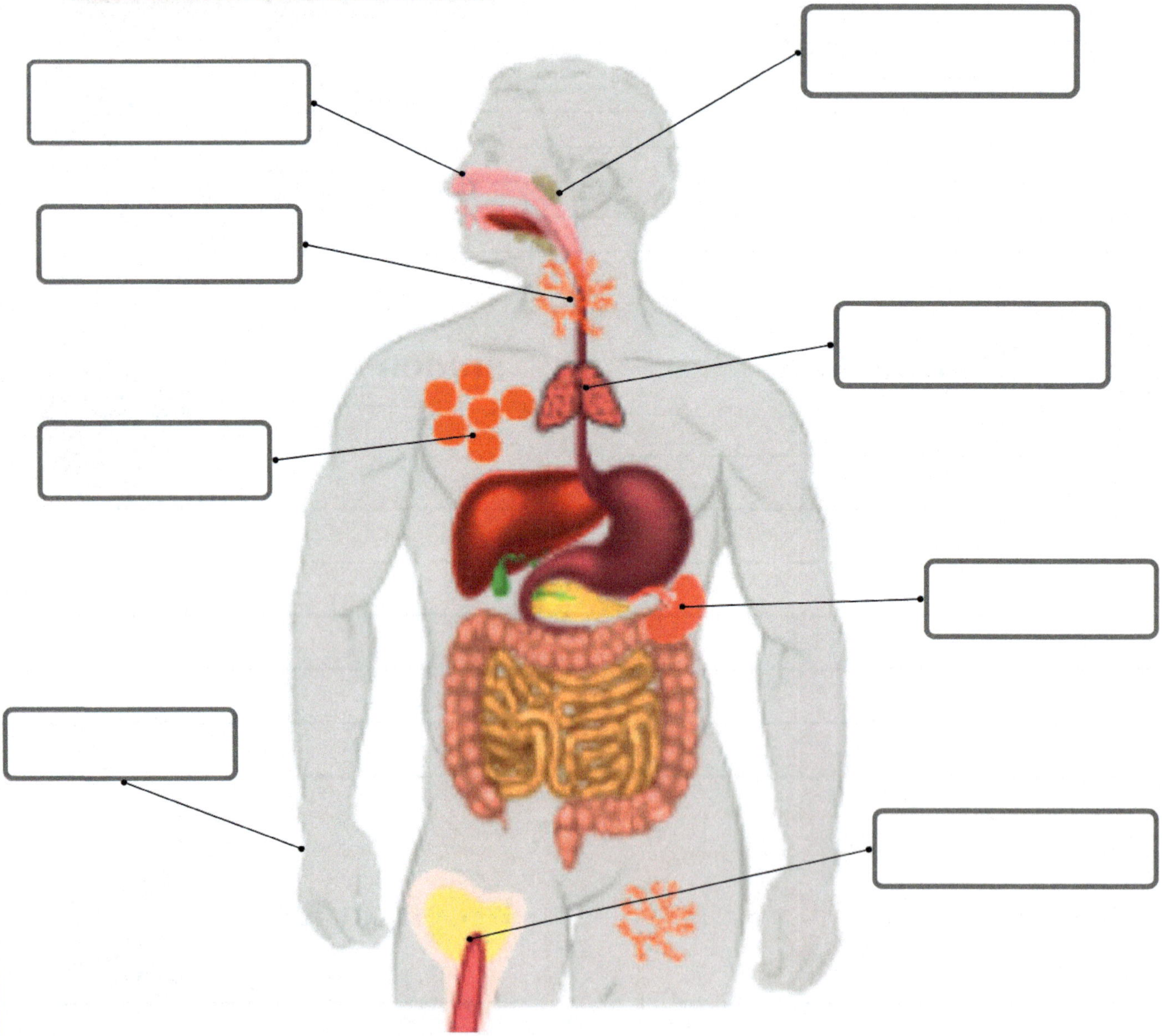

THE IMMUNE SYSTEM

Name:............................... Date:....../....../..........

Parts of the Immune System

LYMPHATIC VESSELS
LYMPH NODES
TONSILS
MUCOUS MEMBRANE
SKIN
SPLEEN
BONE MARROW
THYMUS

THE IMMUNE SYSTEM

Name:................................ Date:....../....../..........

FUNCTIONS:

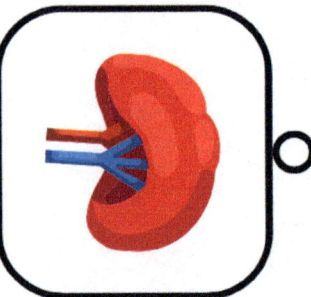 ○———○ FILTER AND TRAP PATHOGENS, TOXINS, AND IMMUNE CELLS TO FACILITATE IMMUNE RESPONSES.

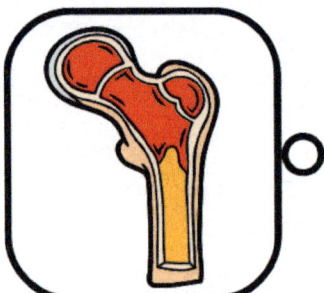 ○———○ STORES PLATELETS, FILTERS BLOOD, AND HELPS IN IMMUNE SURVEILLANCE AND RED BLOOD CELL RECYCLING.

 ○———○ PRODUCES BLOOD CELLS, INCLUDING RED BLOOD CELLS, WHITE BLOOD CELLS, AND PLATELETS.

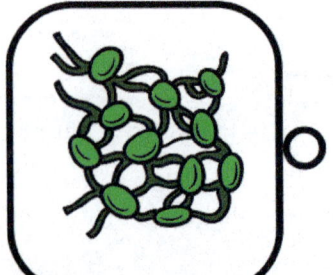 ○———○ MATURATION SITE FOR T LYMPHOCYTES (T CELLS) CRUCIAL FOR ADAPTIVE IMMUNITY.

THE IMMUNE SYSTEM

Name:............................ Date:....../....../.........

The Immune System Diseases:

DISEASES	SYMPTOMS	TREATMENTS
HIV/AIDS		
RHEUMATOID ARTHRITIS		
MULTIPLE SCLEROSIS		
CELIAC DISEASE		
LUPUS		

THE IMMUNE SYSTEM

Name:............................ Date:....../....../........

CHOOSE THE CORRECT ANSWER:

1- What is the primary function of the immune system?

- A) TO REGULATE BODY TEMPERATURE
- B) TO DIGEST FOOD
- C) O DEFEND THE BODY AGAINST PATHOGENS
- D) TO PRODUCE HORMONES

2- Which of the following is NOT a type of white blood cell involved in the immune response?

- A) T LYMPHOCYTE
- B) RED BLOOD CELL
- C) B LYMPHOCYTE
- D) NATURAL KILLER CELL

3- Which component of the immune system is responsible for producing antibodies?

- A) T CELLS
- B) B CELLS
- C) MACROPHAGES
- D) PLATELETS

4- What is the role of antibodies in the immune system?

- A) THEY KILL BACTERIA DIRECTLY
- B) THEY HELP WHITE BLOOD CELLS ENGULF PATHOGENS
- C) THEY NEUTRALIZE PATHOGENS AND MARK THEM FOR DESTRUCTION
- D) THEY STIMULATE THE PRODUCTION OF ANTIGENS

THE IMMUNE SYSTEM

Name:............................. Date:....../....../..........

Choose the correct answer:

5- Which of the following is an example of a non-specific immune response?

| A | ANTIBODY PRODUCTION | B | CYTOTOXIC T-CELL ACTIVATION |
| C | INFLAMMATION | D | MEMORY CELL FORMATION |

6- What is the purpose of vaccines in the context of the immune system?

| A | TO CURE INFECTIONS | B | TO STIMULATE THE PRODUCTION OF ANTIBODIES |
| C | TO DESTROY WHITE BLOOD CELLS | D | TO INHIBIT THE IMMUNE RESPONSE |

7- Which type of immunity is acquired through vaccination or exposure to a disease?

| A | INNATE IMMUNITY | B | PASSIVE IMMUNITY |
| C | ACTIVE IMMUNITY | D | ACQUIRED IMMUNITY |

8- What is the term for the immune system mistakenly attacking the body's own cells and tissues?

| A | IMMUNODEFICIENCY | B | ALLERGY |
| C | AUTOIMMUNITY | D | INFECTION |

THE IMMUNE SYSTEM

ANSWERS:

1- To defend the body against pathogens

2- Red blood cell

3- B cells

4- They neutralize pathogens and mark them for destruction

5- Inflammation

6- To stimulate the production of antibodies

7- Active immunity

8- Autoimmunity

THE URINARY SYSTEM

Name:................................ Date:....../....../..........

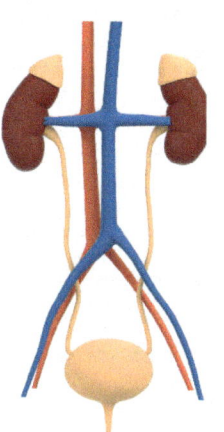

what is the Urinary System
_____
_____
_____
_____
_____

why is it important
_____
_____
_____
_____
_____
_____

kidney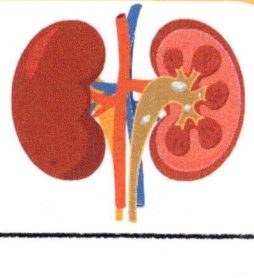
_____
_____
_____
_____
_____
_____

bladder
_____
_____
_____

urethra
_____
_____
_____

69

THE URINARY SYSTEM

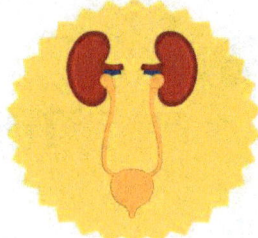

Name:............................... Date:...../...../.........

LABEL THE PARTS BELOW:

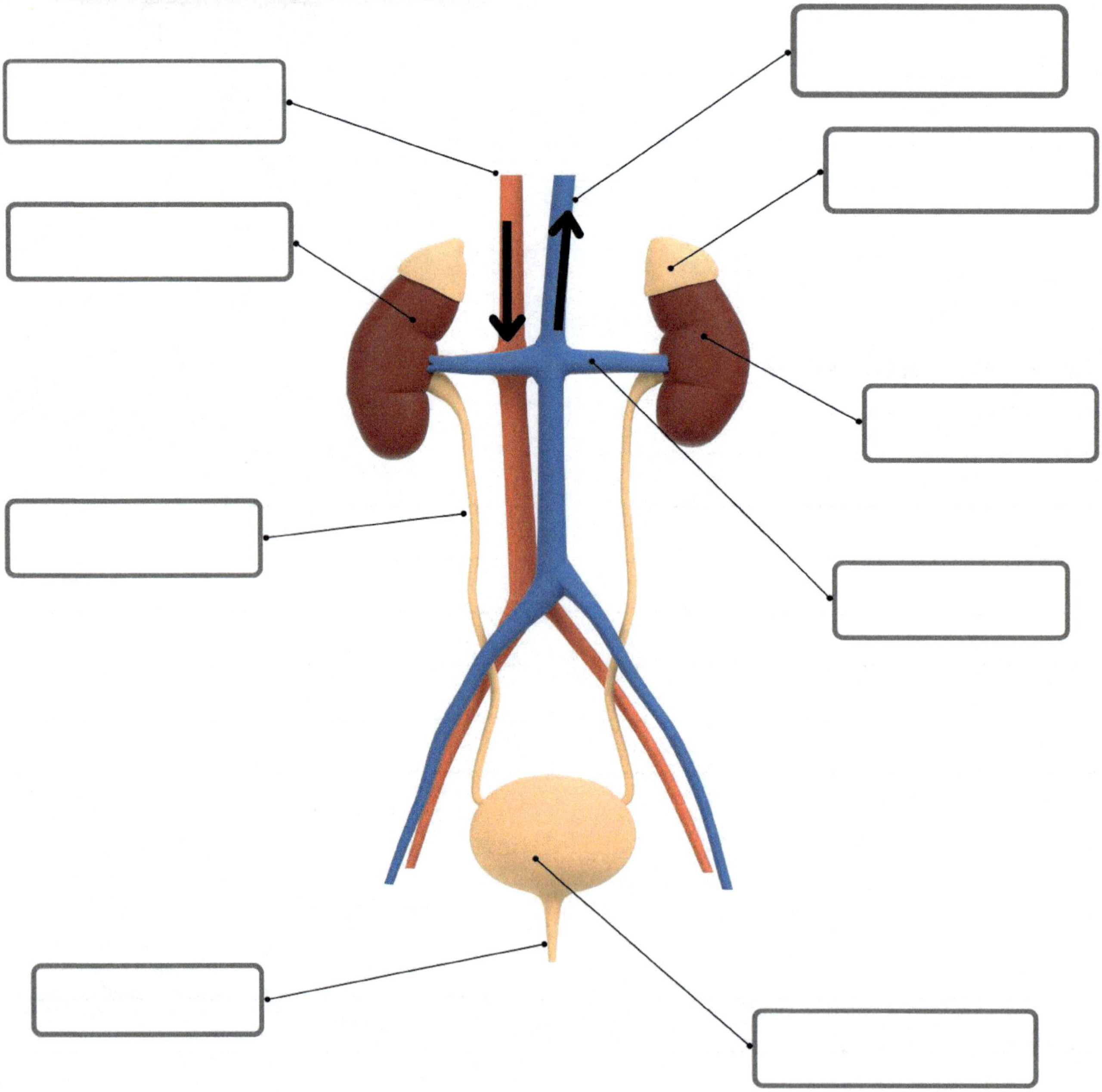

THE URINARY SYSTEM

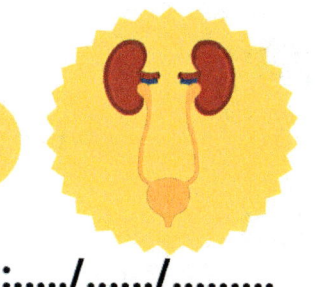

Name:............................ Date:....../....../..........

Parts of the the Urinary System

LEFT KIDNEY
DORSAL AORTA
ADRENAL GLAND
INFERIOR VENA CAVA
RIGHT KIDNEY
RENAL VEIN
URETHRA
URETER
BLADDER

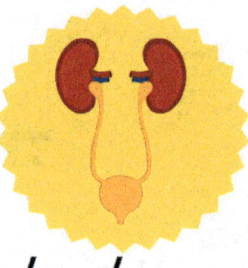

THE URINARY SYSTEM

Name:............................ Date:....../....../........

Functions:

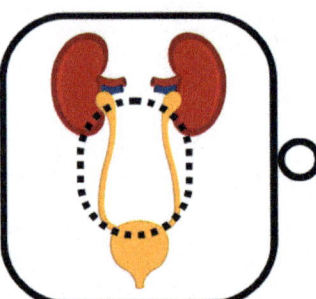

STORES URINE UNTIL IT'S READY FOR ELIMINATION.

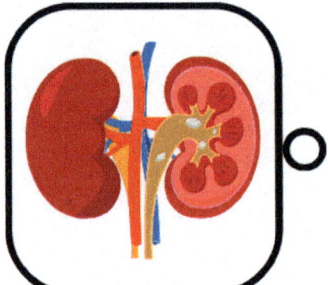

TRANSPORTS URINE FROM THE KIDNEYS TO THE BLADDER.

PASSAGEWAY FOR URINE TO EXIT THE BODY FROM THE BLADDER.

FILTERS BLOOD TO REMOVE WASTE AND EXCESS FLUID, FORMING URINE.

THE URINARY SYSTEM

Name:................................ Date:....../....../..........

The Urinary System Diseases:

DISEASES	SYMPTOMS	TREATMENTS
URINARY TRACT INFECTION		
KIDNEY STONES		
BLADDER INFECTIONS		
KIDNEY DISEASE		
INTERSTITIAL CYSTITIS		

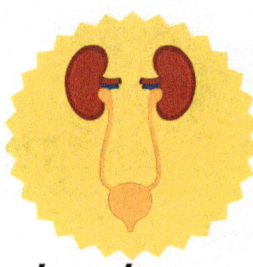

THE URINARY SYSTEM

Name:...........................   Date:...../...../..........

Choose the correct answer:

1- What is the primary function of the urinary system?

- A DIGESTION
- B RESPIRATION
- C FILTRATION AND EXCRETION OF WASTE PRODUCTS
- D REPRODUCTION

2- Which of the following organs is NOT a part of the urinary system?

- A KIDNEYS
- B BLADDER
- C LIVER
- D URETERS

3- Which of the following is the functional unit of the kidney responsible for filtering blood and forming urine?

- A NEPHRON
- B URETHRA
- C URETER
- D RENAL CORTEX

4- The tube that carries urine from the kidney to the bladder is called the:

- A URETHRA
- B URETER
- C NEPHRON
- D BLADDER

THE URINARY SYSTEM

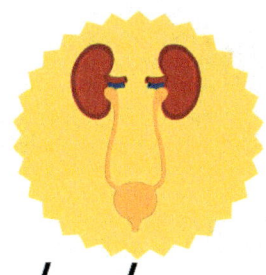

Name:............................ Date:...../...../........

Choose the correct answer:

5- What is the name of the hormone produced by the kidneys that helps regulate blood pressure and the production of red blood cells?

| A | INSULIN | B | THYROXINE |
| C | RENIN | D | MELATONIN |

6- Which of the following substances is typically not found in urine?

| A | GLUCOSE | B | UREA |
| C | CREATININE | D | SODIUM |

7- What is the normal color of urine in a healthy individual?

| A | BLUE | B | GREEN |
| C | YELLOW | D | RED |

8- Which of the following conditions is characterized by the inflammation of the bladder, often resulting in frequent and painful urination?

| A | KIDNEY STONES | B | URINARY TRACT INFECTION |
| C | DIABETES | D | HEMATURIA |

THE URINARY SYSTEM
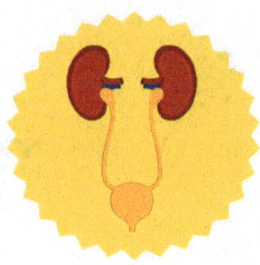

ANSWERS:

1- Filtration and excretion of waste products

2- Liver

3- Nephron

4- Ureter

5- Renin

6- Glucose

7- Yellow

8- Urinary tract infection

THE INTEGUMENTARY SYSTEM

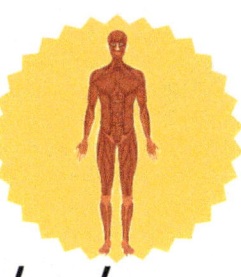

Name:............................ Date:...../...../.........

what is the Integumentary System
_____
_____
_____
_____
_____

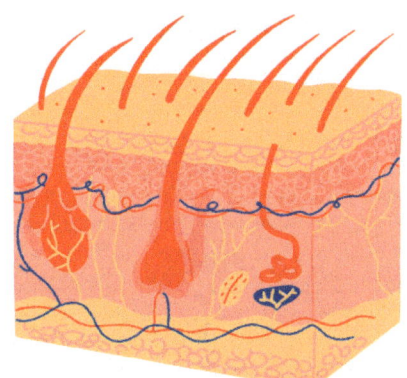

why is it important
_____
_____
_____
_____
_____
_____

Skin
_____
_____
_____
_____
_____
_____

Hair
_____
_____
_____
_____

Nails
_____
_____
_____
_____

THE INTEGUMENTARY SYSTEM

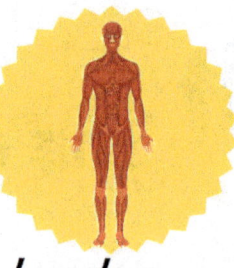

Name:............................... Date:....../....../.........

Label the parts below:

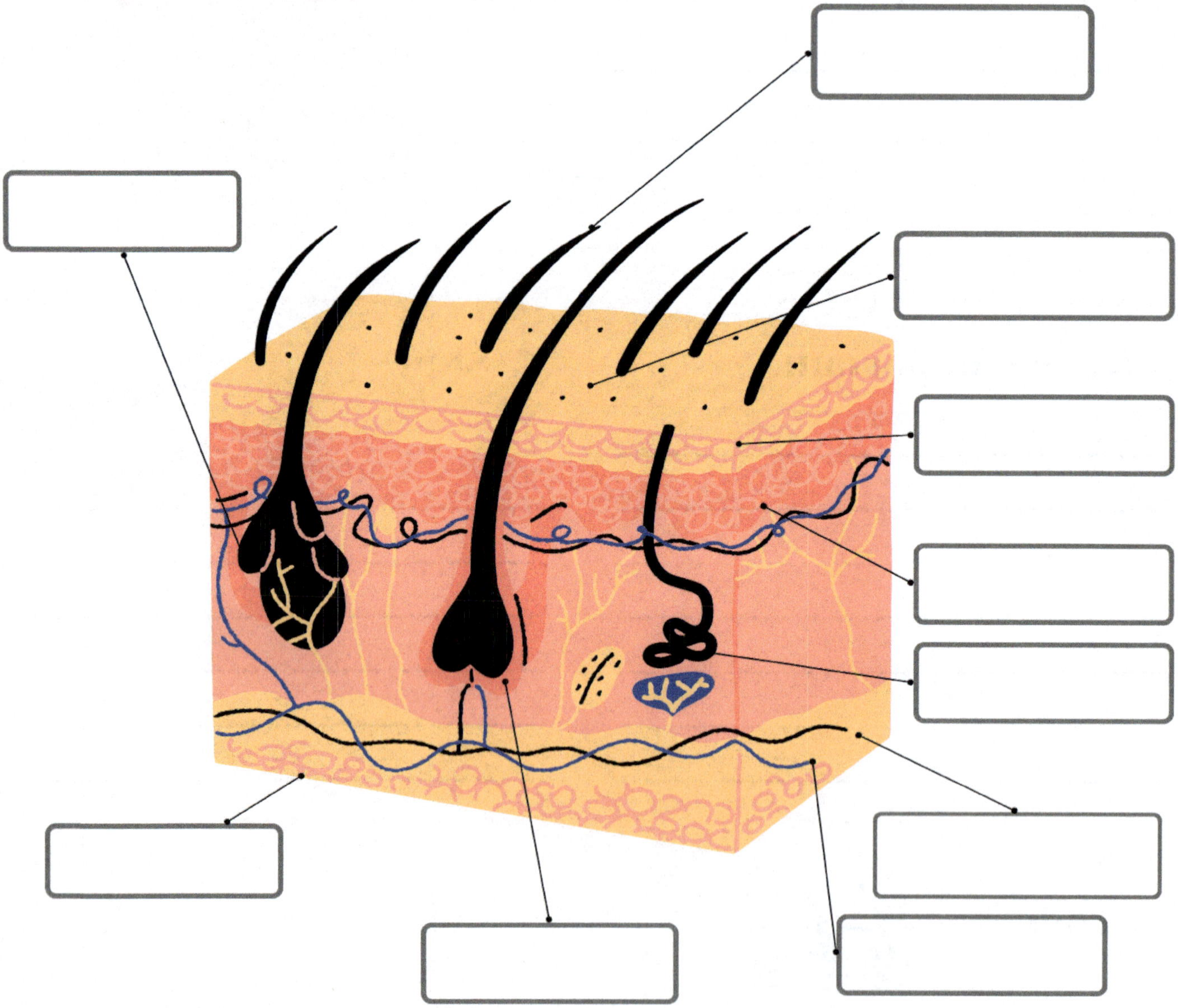

78

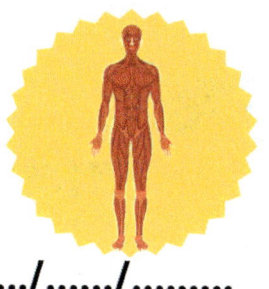

THE INTEGUMENTARY SYSTEM

Name:................................ Date:....../....../.........

Parts of the Integumentary System

ARTERY
PORES
SWEAT PORES
STRATUM CORNEUM
HAIR SHAFT
SQUAMOUS CELLS
SEBACEOUS GLAND
VEIN
HAIR FOLLICLE
ADIPOSE TISSUE

THE INTEGUMENTARY SYSTEM

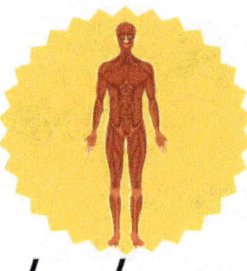

Name:............................ Date:....../....../..........

Functions:

PROVIDE PROTECTION TO THE FINGERTIPS AND ENHANCE FINE MOTOR SKILLS; THEY ARE ALSO USED FOR SCRATCHING AND PICKING UP SMALL OBJECTS.

PRODUCE AND SECRETE SEBUM, AN OILY SUBSTANCE THAT HELPS MOISTURIZE AND PROTECT THE SKIN AND HAIR.

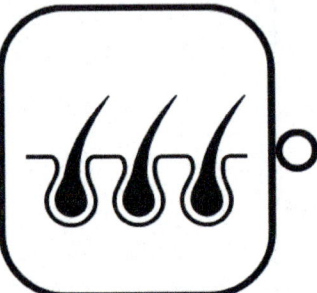

ACTS AS A PROTECTIVE BARRIER AGAINST EXTERNAL THREATS, REGULATES BODY TEMPERATURE, AND HOUSES SENSORY RECEPTORS FOR TOUCH, PAIN, AND TEMPERATURE.

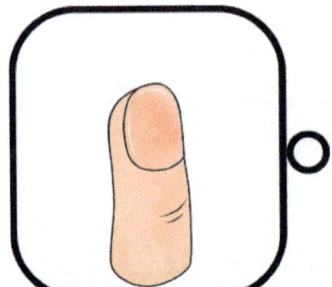

SERVES AS INSULATION AND PROTECTION FOR THE SCALP, HELPS REGULATE BODY TEMPERATURE, AND PLAYS A ROLE IN SENSORY PERCEPTION, SUCH AS DETECTING TOUCH AND ENVIRONMENTAL CHANGES.

THE INTEGUMENTARY SYSTEM

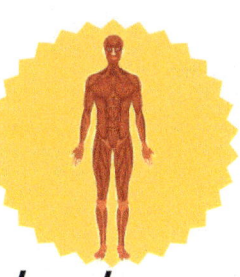

Name:................................ Date:......./......./..........

The Integumentary System Diseases:

DISEASES	SYMPTOMS	TREATMENTS
PSORIASIS		
ACNE		
ECZEMA		
SKIN CANCER		
HERPES ZOSTER		

THE INTEGUMENTARY SYSTEM
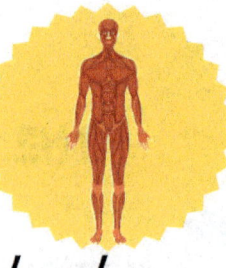

Name:............................ Date:....../....../..........

CHOOSE THE CORRECT ANSWER:

1- What is the primary function of the integumentary system?

- A. TRANSPORTATION OF NUTRIENTS
- B. PROTECTION FROM EXTERNAL THREATS
- C. REGULATION OF BODY TEMPERATURE
- D. FILTERING OF WASTE PRODUCTS

2- Which layer of the skin contains sweat glands, hair follicles, and sebaceous glands?

- A. EPIDERMIS
- B. DERMIS
- C. HYPODERMIS
- D. SUBCUTANEOUS LAYER

3- What pigment gives human skin its color and provides some protection against UV radiation?

- A. CAROTENE
- B. MELANIN
- C. HEMOGLOBIN
- D. COLLAGEN

4- Which of the following is not a common function of sweat produced by sweat glands in the skin?

- A. COOLING THE BODY
- B. ELIMINATING WASTE PRODUCTS
- C. MOISTURIZING THE SKIN
- D. PROTECTING AGAINST PATHOGENS

THE INTEGUMENTARY SYSTEM

Name:............................ Date:....../....../..........

CHOOSE THE CORRECT ANSWER:

5- What condition results from the inflammation and infection of a hair follicle or sweat gland?

- A ACNE
- B ECZEMA
- C PSORIASIS
- D DERMATITIS

6- The outermost layer of the epidermis primarily consists of:

- A KERATINOCYTES
- B MELANOCYTES
- C LANGERHANS CELLS
- D MERKEL CELLS

7- Which vitamin is synthesized by the skin when exposed to sunlight?

- A VITAMIN A
- B VITAMIN B12
- C VITAMIN C
- D VITAMIN D

8- What is the medical term for the loss of hair, especially from the scalp?

- A ALOPECIA
- B ECZEMA
- C PSORIASIS
- D MELANOMA

THE INTEGUMENTARY SYSTEM

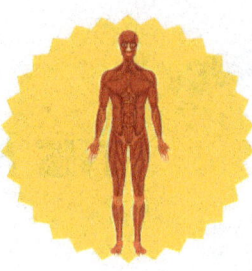

ANSWERS:

1-Protection from external threats

2-Dermis

3-Melanin

4-Moisturizing the skin

5-Acne

6-Keratinocytes

7-Vitamin D

8-Alopecia

THE REPRODUCTIVE SYSTEM

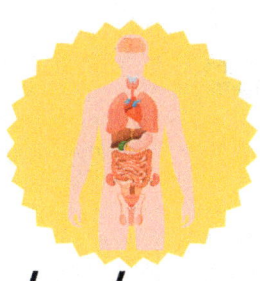

Name:............................   Date:....../....../.........

what is the Reproductive System
_____
_____
_____
_____
_____
_____

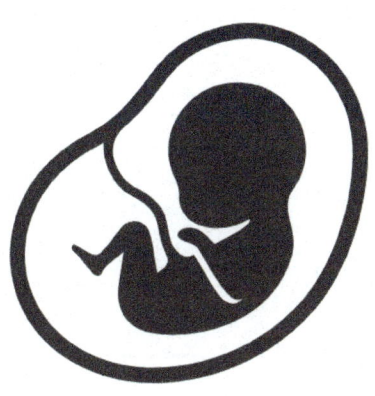

why is it important
_____
_____
_____
_____
_____
_____

Pregnancy
_____
_____
_____
_____
_____
_____

testils
_____
_____
_____
_____

ovary
_____
_____
_____
_____

THE REPRODUCTIVE SYSTEM

Name:............................ Date:....../....../........

LABEL THE PARTS BELOW:

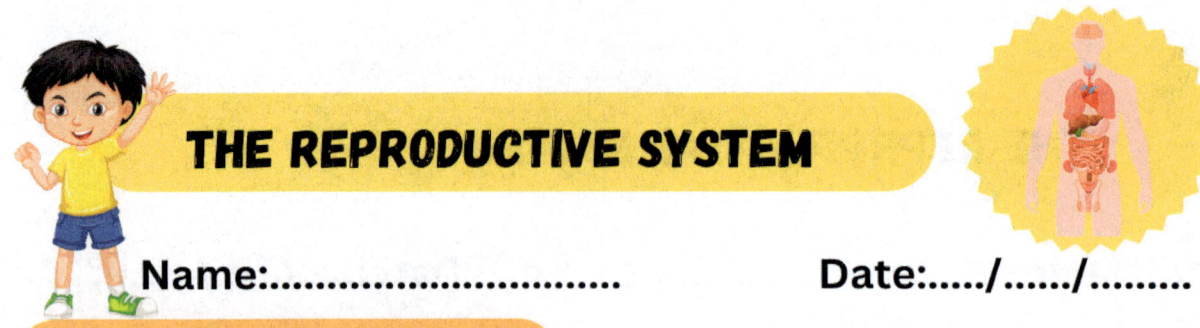

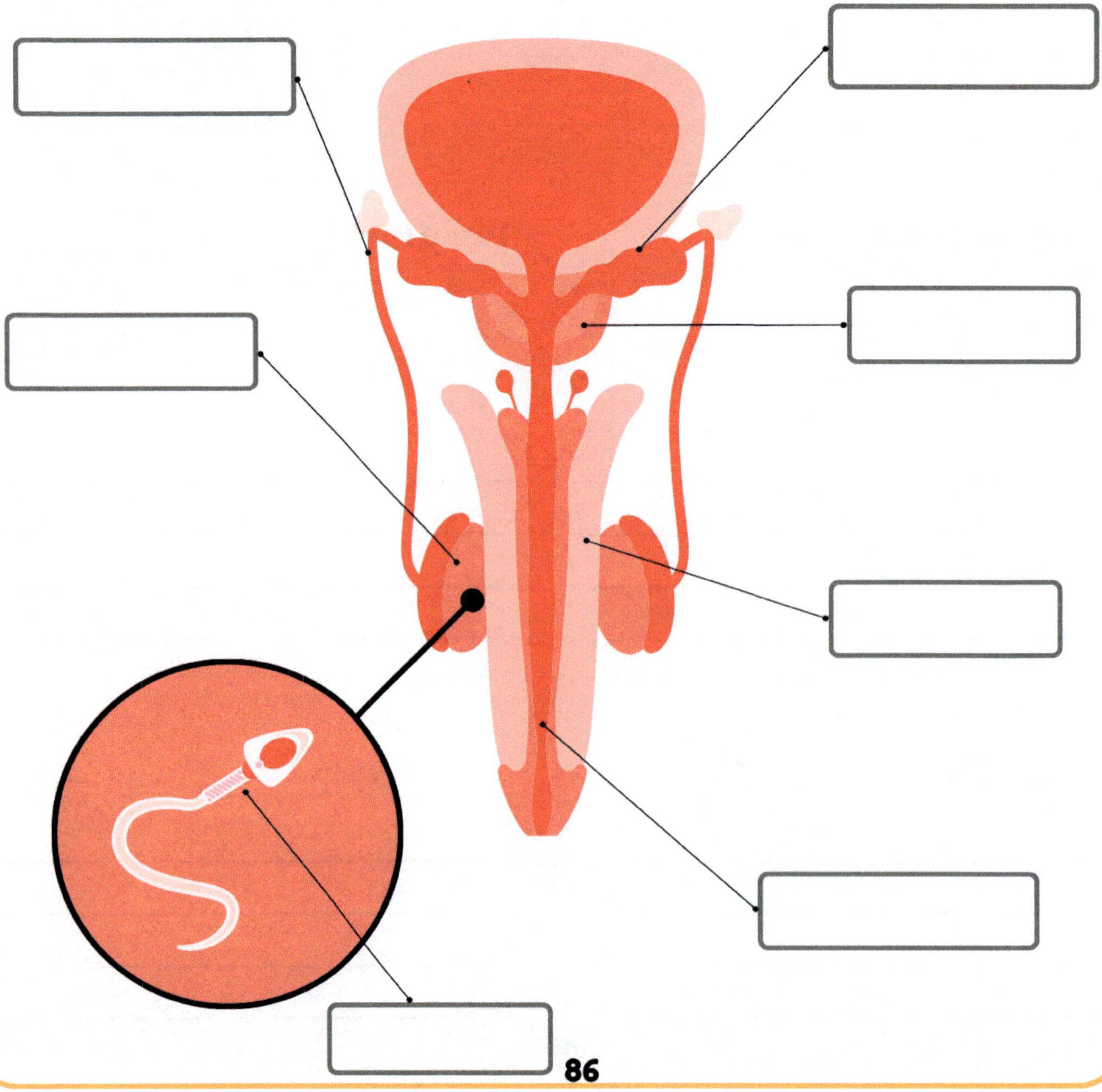

THE REPRODUCTIVE SYSTEM

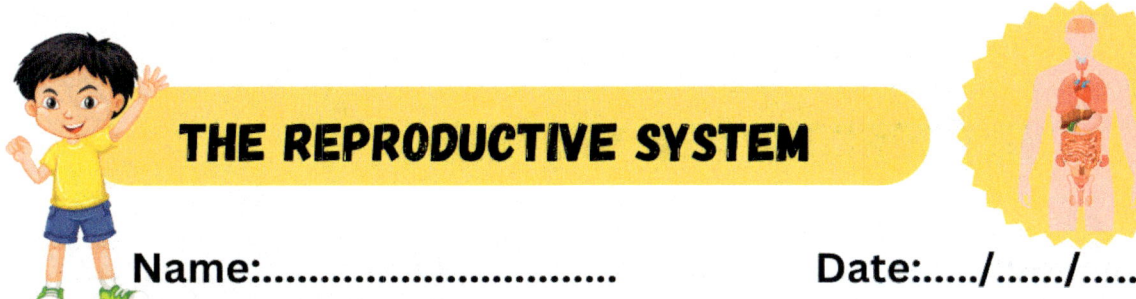

Name:................................ Date:...../...../.........

LABEL THE PARTS BELOW:

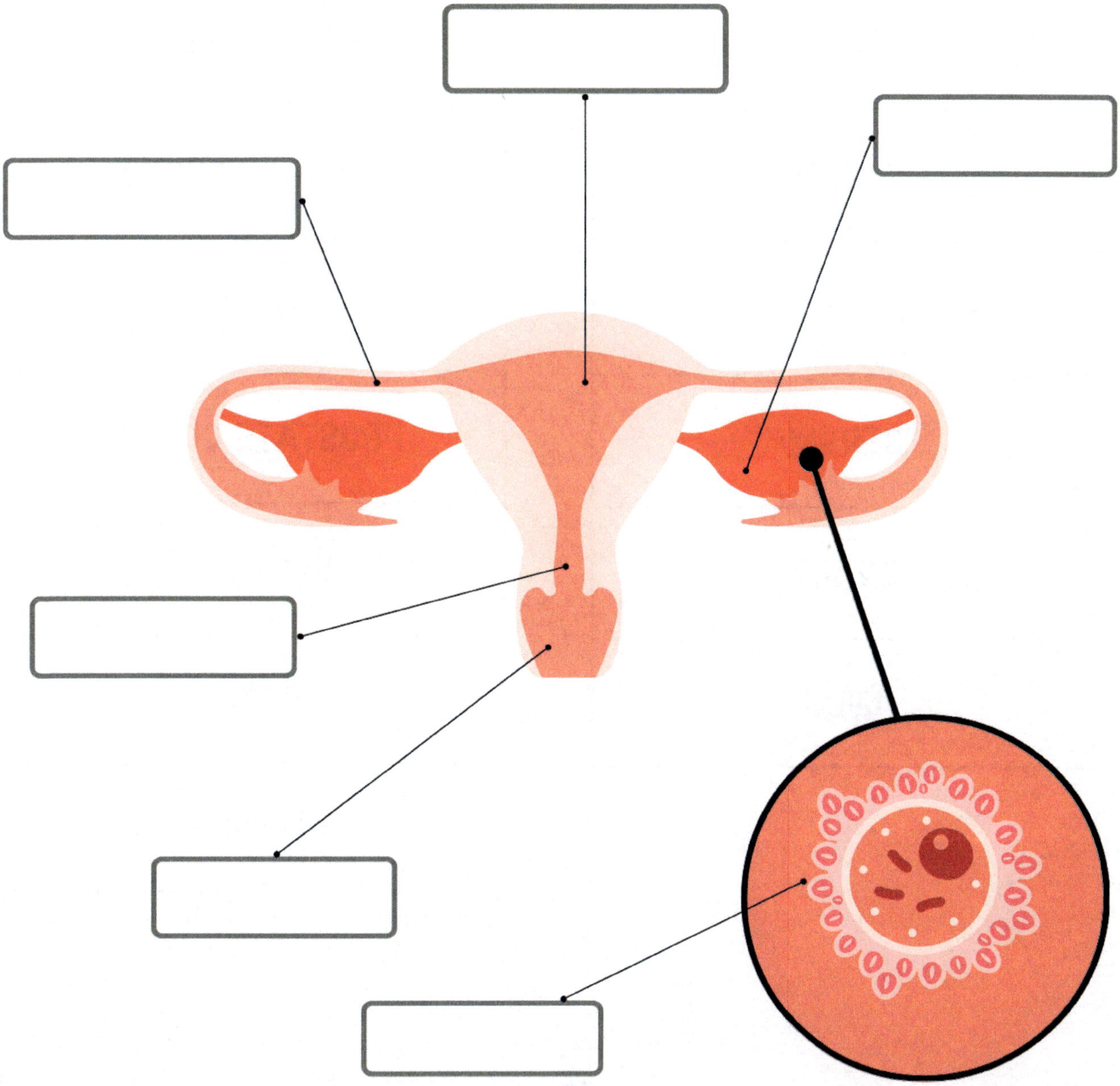

87

THE REPRODUCTIVE SYSTEM

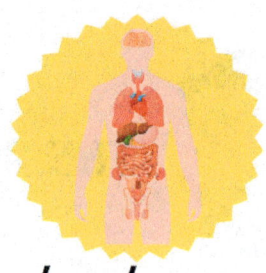

Name:............................ Date:....../....../........

Parts of the reproductive system

female

UTERUS
VAGINA
FALLOPIAN TUBE
CERVIX
OVARY
OVUM

male

VAS DEFERENS
SEMINAL VESICLE
PENIS
PROSTATE GLAND
URETHRA
TESTIS
SPERM

THE REPRODUCTIVE SYSTEM

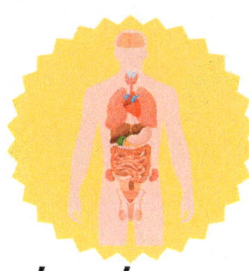

Name:............................   Date:...../...../.........

Functions:

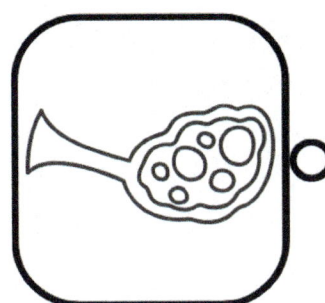

PRODUCING SPERM AND SECRETING TESTOSTERONE, A HORMONE CRUCIAL FOR MALE SEXUAL DEVELOPMENT AND SECONDARY SEXUAL CHARACTERISTICS.

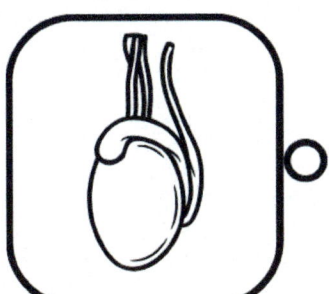

IS THE FEMALE REPRODUCTIVE CELL (GAMETE) THAT, WHEN FERTILIZED BY SPERM, FORMS A ZYGOTE, WHICH DEVELOPS INTO AN EMBRYO, ULTIMATELY LEADING TO THE FORMATION OF A NEW ORGANISM.

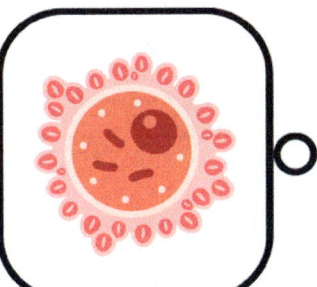

MALE REPRODUCTIVE CELLS (GAMETES) DESIGNED FOR FERTILIZATION, CARRYING GENETIC MATERIAL FROM THE MALE TO COMBINE WITH THE FEMALE'S EGG (OVUM) DURING FERTILIZATION.

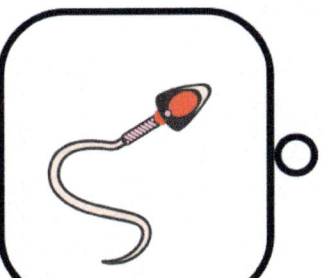

IS AN ESSENTIAL FEMALE REPRODUCTIVE ORGAN THAT PRODUCES AND RELEASES OVUM (EGGS) DURING THE MENSTRUAL CYCLE, AND IT ALSO PRODUCES HORMONES LIKE ESTROGEN AND PROGESTERONE, WHICH REGULATE THE FEMALE REPRODUCTIVE SYSTEM AND SECONDARY SEXUAL CHARACTERISTICS.

THE REPRODUCTIVE SYSTEM

Name:............................. Date:....../....../........

THE REPRODUCTIVE SYSTEM Diseases:

DISEASES	SYMPTOMS	TREATMENTS
POLYCYSTIC OVARY SYNDROME		
ENDOMETRIOSIS		
PROSTATE CANCER		
INFERTILITY		
PELVIC INFLAMMATORY DISEASE		

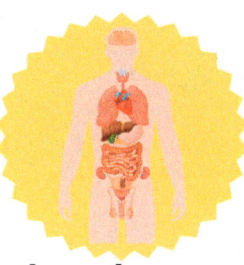

THE REPRODUCTIVE SYSTEM

Name:............................ Date:...../....../........

Choose the correct answer:

1- What is the primary function of the male reproductive system?

- A PRODUCING EGGS
- B PRODUCING SPERM
- C NURTURING THE DEVELOPING FETUS
- D OVULATION

2- Where does fertilization typically occur in the human reproductive system?

- A UTERUS
- B FALLOPIAN TUBE
- C VAGINA
- D OVARY

3- Which hormone is primarily responsible for regulating the menstrual cycle in females?

- A ESTROGEN
- B PROGESTERONE
- C TESTOSTERONE
- D PROLACTIN

4- What is the role of the epididymis in the male reproductive system?

- A PRODUCING SPERM
- B STORING AND MATURING SPERM
- C TRANSPORTING EGGS TO THE UTERUS
- D PRODUCING TESTOSTERONE

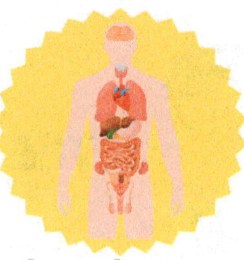

THE REPRODUCTIVE SYSTEM

Name:............................ Date:....../....../........

CHOOSE THE CORRECT ANSWER:

5- Which female reproductive organ is responsible for nurturing and supporting a developing embryo or fetus during pregnancy?

- **A** OVARY
- **B** FALLOPIAN TUBE
- **C** UTERUS
- **D** VAGINA

6- What is the process by which the fertilized egg implants itself into the uterine wall?

- **A** OVULATION
- **B** MENSTRUATION
- **C** FERTILIZATION
- **D** IMPLANTATION

7- Which sexually transmitted infection (STI) can lead to cervical cancer in females?

- **A** GONORRHEA
- **B** CHLAMYDIA
- **C** HUMAN PAPILLOMAVIRUS (HPV)
- **D** SYPHILIS

8- In the male reproductive system, what is the function of the prostate gland?

- **A** PRODUCING SPERM
- **B** PRODUCING TESTOSTERONE
- **C** PRODUCING SEMINAL FLUID
- **D** TRANSPORTING SPERM TO THE URETHRA

 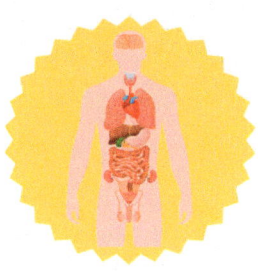

THE REPRODUCTIVE SYSTEM

ANSWERS:

1- Producing sperm

2- Fallopian tube

3- Estrogen

4- Storing and maturing sperm

5- Uterus

6- Implantation

7- Human papillomavirus (HPV)

8- Producing seminal fluid

Printed in Great Britain
by Amazon

59252430R10053